Mastering Shell for DevOps

Automate, streamline, and secure DevOps workflows with modern shell scripting

Gilbert Stew

Published by: GitforGits

Publisher: Sonal Dhandre

www.gitforgits.com

support@gitforgits.com

Printed in India

First Printing: November 2024

ISBN: 978-81-979504-2-1

Cover Design by: Kitten Publishing

Prologue

When I first started working in the DevOps field, it was pretty overwhelming. There were a lot of repetitive tasks and manual configurations to deal with. Every deployment felt like starting from scratch, and the slightest mistake could cause major problems with the system. Without automation, my team and I spent a lot of time on tasks that should have been simple. We were more often than not just putting out fires and not innovating, and it was pretty frustrating.

One day, after a particularly rough week of manual deployments and unexpected system failures, I realized there had to be a better way. I started looking into shell scripting. It was like opening a whole new world in DevOps. All of a sudden, we could automate repetitive tasks, cut down on errors, and save a lot of time. The command line became my canvas, where I could script out solutions to problems that once seemed impossible.

As I started using shell scripting in our workflows, I could see a real change. Deployments were more reliable, configuration drift was reduced, and our systems were more resilient. My team went from being reactive to proactive, focusing on optimization rather than just maintenance. The beauty of shell scripts is that they make it simple and elegant to link up different tools and platforms.

This book is where I've reached the end of my journey from struggling with manual DevOps to feeling empowered by mastering shell scripting. I wrote it to share the practical knowledge and insights I've gained, in the hope that it'll help others to navigate the complexities of DevOps with greater ease. If we use shell to its fullest, we can automate, innovate, and take our practices to the next level.

Content

Preface xii

GitforGits xiii

Acknowledgement xiv

Chapter 1: Automating Routine DevOps Tasks 1

Overview 2

Up and Running with Shell Automation 2

Getting Started with Bash Scripting 3
Add Flexibility Parameters 4
Run Scripts on Schedule 5
Bash Variables for Enhanced Customization 5

Creating Reusable Scripts 6

Build Modular Script with Functions 6
Run Multiple Tasks in One Execution 8
Add Optional Logging 9

Error Handling and Logging 11

Scenario 1: Handle Command Not Found Errors 12
Scenario 2: Handle Permission Denied Errors 13
Scenario 3: Handle Missing/Non-Existent files 13
Scenario 4: Handle Unexpected Input 14

Knowledge Exercise 15

Chapter 2: Managing CI/CD Pipelines with Shell Scripting 20

Overview 21

Automating CI/CD Pipeline Steps 21

Setting up Project Structure 21
Create the Build Script 22
Create Test Script 22
Create Deployment Script 23
Create CI/CD Pipeline Script 24
Execute CI/CD Pipeline 25

Integrating with Jenkins and GitLab CI 25

Integrate with Jenkins 25

Integrate with GitLab CI 27
Interact with CI/CD Tool APIs 28
Monitor Pipeline Status 29

Scripted Code Rollbacks and Redeployments 29
Implement Version Control with Git Tags 30
Enhance Deployment Script 30
Create Rollback Script 31
Integrate Rollback Logic into Pipeline 32
Handle Configuration and Database Changes 33
Add Notifications, Logging and Fixing Issues 33

Summary 34

CHAPTER 3: TEST AUTOMATION AND VALIDATION SCRIPTS 35

Overview 36

Writing Automated Unit and Integration Test Scripts 36
Setting up Testing Framework 36
Create Test Script 37
Define Test Scripts 37
Incorporate Environment Variables 38
Generate Test Reports 39
Handle Test Databases 40
Parallelize Tests 42
Integrate Tests into CI/CD Pipeline 42

Automating Code Quality Checks 43
Setting up Linting Tools 44
Create Linting Script 44
Configure ESLint Rules 44
Integrate Static Analysis Tools 45
Update Test Script with Code Quality Checks 45
Generate Code Quality Reports 46
Integrate Code Quality Checks into the CI/CD Pipeline 47
Automate Code Formatting 48
Enforce Commit Standards with Husky 48

Dynamic Validation with Shell Scripts 49
Validate Application Health 49
Validate API Endpoints 50
Validate Response Content 50
Validate Infrastructure Components 51
Aggregate Validation Checks 52
Integrate Validation into Deployment Workflow 53
Schedule Regular Validation 54

Send Alerts on Failure ... 54

Summary ... *54*

CHAPTER 4: TASK SCHEDULING AND MONITORING WITH CRONTAB ... 56

Overview ... *57*

Setting up Scheduled Tasks ... *57*

Understand CRONTAB Syntax ... 57
Setting up Backups with CRONTAB ... 58
Automate Health Checks ... 58
Schedule Log Rotations ... 58
Using Environment Variables in CRON Jobs ... 59
Schedule Jobs with Special Timing Needs ... 59
Using System-Wide CRON Directories ... 60

Monitoring Scheduled Tasks ... *60*

Create a Monitor Script ... 60
Schedule Monitor Script ... 61
Implement Alert Notifications ... 62
Create a Dashboard for CRON Jobs ... 63
Implement Retry Mechanisms ... 63

Dynamic Scheduling and CRON Alternatives ... *64*

Using 'at' Command ... 64
Leveraging 'anacron' for Infrequent Tasks ... 65
Advanced Schedule with 'systemd' Timers ... 65
Utilize 'batch' Command ... 66
Event-Driven Schedule with 'inotify' ... 66
Implement Flexible Schedule with 'fcron' ... 67

Summary ... *67*

Chapter 5: Orchestrating Infrastructure with Shell Scripting ... 68

Overview ... *69*

Automating Infrastructure Setup and Tear-Down ... *69*

Provision Servers ... 69
Configure Server Automatically ... 71
Automate Infrastructure Teardown ... 72
Automate Entire Workflow ... 73

Scripting Configuration Management Tasks ... *74*

Automate Configuration File Management ... 75
Automate Environment Setup ... 76
Automate Software Deployment ... 76
Automate User and Permission Management ... 77

Automate Firewall Configuration 77
Automate Environment Consistency across Multiple Servers 78
Automate with Infrastructure as Code Tools 79

Version Control and Documentation of Infrastructure Scripts 80
Using Git 80
Document Infrastructure Scripts 81
Leverage Git Hooks for Quality Control 83

Summary 83

CHAPTER 6: INCIDENT RESOLUTION AND LOG MANAGEMENT 85

Overview 86

Automating Incident Detection and Alerts 86
Why Automation in Incident Detection? 86
Monitor System Metrics 86
Detect Service Status 88
Automate Alert Triggers 88
Implement Threshold-Based Alerts 89
Integrate with Monitor Tools 90

Quick Incident Resolution Scripts 90
Automate Service Restarts 90
Automate Resource Allocation 91
Automate Log Clearance 92
Automate Database Maintenance 92
Integrate Incident Resolution Scripts with Detection 93
Automate User Session Management 93

Automating Log Collection and Analysis 94
Collect Logs from Multiple Sources 94
Parse Logs for Meaningful Data 95
Automate Log Management Process 96

Summary 97

CHAPTER 7: MANAGING NETWORK TRAFFIC AND LOAD BALANCING 98

Overview 99

Traffic Monitoring with Shell Scripts 99
Implement Network Traffic Monitoring 99
Visualize and Log Inbound and Outbound Traffic 101
Automate Continuous Monitoring 102

Automating Load Balancer Configuration 104
Understand the Need for Automation 104

Setting up HAProxy 104
Configure HAProxy Manually 104
Automate Backend Server Updates 105
Automate Scale Based on Traffic Load 107
Implement Auto Scale Policies 108
Automate Load Balancer Configuration in Cloud 110
Integrate with Configuration Management Tools 111

Failover and Traffic Redirection Scripts *113*
Implement Failover with HAProxy 113
Implement DNS-Based Failover 115
IP Routing Failover with 'Keepalived' 117
Automate Failover Actions 118

Summary *118*

CHAPTER 8: CONTAINERIZATION AND SHELL SCRIPTING **120**

Overview *121*

Container Deployment with Docker and Podman *121*
Install Docker 121
Install Podman 122
Automate Container Deployment with Docker 123
Automate Container Deployment with Podman 126
Configure Environment Variables 129
Automate Container Deployment across Environments 130

Managing Containers and Orchestration *131*
Scale Containers 131
Access Container Logs 133
Implement Health Checks 134
Manage Container Networking 134
Implement Load Balancing 135
Monitor Containers 137

Automating Kubernetes Deployment and Management *138*
Install kubectl 138
Setting up a Kubernetes Cluster 139
Deploy Applications with 'kubectl' 140
Automate Updates 142
Automate Rollbacks 143
Automate Health Checks 143
Automate Resource Management 144
Automate CI/CD Integration 144

Summary *145*

CHAPTER 9: DEVOPS SECURITY AUTOMATION WITH SHELL SCRIPTING **147**

Overview ***148***

Scripting User Access and Permissions Management ***148***

Automate User Account Setup 148
Automate Permission Assignment 150
Automate Access Control 152
Automate User Deactivation and Removal 152
Automate SSH Key Management 154
Automate Password Policy Enforcement 155
Automate Audit of User Accounts 156

Automating Vulnerability Scanning and Patching ***156***

Automate Security Scans 157
Automate Vulnerability Checks 158
Automate Patch Deployment 159
Automate Notifications 159
Automate System Reboots After Patching 160
Automate Vulnerability Scanning for Containers 161
Automate Log Monitor for Security Events 161
Automate Firewall Configuration 162
Automate Security Policy Enforcement 163

System Audits and Compliance Checks ***164***

Overview 164
Using OpenSCAP for Compliance Checks 164
Automate Configuration Verification 166
Collect System Configuration Data 167
Compare Configurations Against Baselines 168
Schedule Regular Audits 170
Secure Audit Data 170

Summary ***170***

Index ***172***

Epilogue ***174***

Preface

"Mastering Shell for DevOps" is all about giving DevOps, cloud, and Linux folks the know-how to automate and make their workflows more efficient with shell scripting. The book uses real-world examples and simple instructions to show how to automate tasks and move away from manual work in a DevOps environment.

We start with the basics of shell scripting, so you can learn to write scripts that get the job done. It then moves on to version control with Git and GitHub, showing the importance of collaboration and code management in this context. The book then jumps into infrastructure provisioning and configuration management, showing you how to automate the setup of servers and services using tools like AWS CLI, Docker, and Kubernetes.

As your skills grow, you'll learn to set up monitoring and logging tools, automate incident detection and resolution, and manage network traffic and load balancing. The book also helps you learn how to automate security tasks, including user access management, vulnerability scanning, patching, and compliance checks. By the end of the book, you'll have a whole toolkit of shell scripts that will help you work more efficiently, reliably, and securely in your DevOps practices.

In this book you will:

- Get your infrastructure provisioning done automatically with shell scripts for reliable, fast deployments.
- Make version control a lot easier by using Git and shell scripting for collaborative development.
- Set up a system to monitor and log your data automatically so you can spot any issues early on.
- Make it easy to spot and fix problems so your system stays up and running.
- Get the most out of your network traffic and load balancing with shell scripts for top performance.
- You can deploy and manage containers with Docker, Podman, and Kubernetes using automation.
- Give security a boost with scripted access management and permission assignments.
- Automate vulnerability scanning and patching to keep your system secure.
- Run system audits and compliance checks with scripted automation.

GitforGits

Prerequisites

This book is for DevOps folks, Linux admins, cloud pros, and networking administrators who are looking to make the most out of shell scripting in managing DevOps in a smooth and seamless way. If you have some background in shell scripting and devops, you'll find this book more useful.

Codes Usage

Are you in need of some helpful code examples to assist you in your programming and documentation? Look no further! Our book offers a wealth of supplemental material, including code examples and exercises.

Not only is this book here to aid you in getting your job done, but you have our permission to use the example code in your programs and documentation. However, please note that if you are reproducing a significant portion of the code, we do require you to contact us for permission.

But don't worry, using several chunks of code from this book in your program or answering a question by citing our book and quoting example code does not require permission. But if you do choose to give credit, an attribution typically includes the title, author, publisher, and ISBN. For example, "Mastering Shell for DevOps by Gilbert Stew".

If you are unsure whether your intended use of the code examples falls under fair use or the permissions outlined above, please do not hesitate to reach out to us at support@gitforgits.com.

We are happy to assist and clarify any concerns.

Acknowledgement

I'm really grateful to GitforGits for their amazing support and advice throughout the writing of this book. Thanks to their expertise and attention to detail, the book is suitable for readers of all levels and abilities. I'd also like to thank everyone involved in the publishing process for all their hard work in making this book a reality. From copyediting to advertising, their efforts made the project what it is today.

And finally, I'd like to thank everyone who has shown me unconditional love and encouragement throughout my life. They were a huge help in getting this book finished. I really appreciate your help with this project and your ongoing interest in my career.

CHAPTER 1: AUTOMATING ROUTINE DEVOPS TASKS

Overview

In this chapter, we will go over the key skills and techniques you need to automate your daily DevOps tasks with Bash scripting. We will start with the essentials of shell automation, and you will see how Bash can cut out all those manual tasks and make your workflows more efficient. When you automate those repetitive actions, you will not only reduce errors but also streamline your work processes. This makes things more consistent and easier to manage in different environments.

Next, we will look at how to create scripts that can be used in different ways. Instead of writing one script for each task, you will learn to build scripts that can handle a range of tasks through modular design. This flexibility means you can adapt your automation workflows without starting from scratch each time. This makes your system more efficient and scalable, so you can handle different DevOps requirements.

Finally, we will look at how to handle errors and log information in scripts to make them more reliable. Here, we will look at how to design scripts to deal with potential problems, capture the right info, and keep a clear log of what's going on. Having a solid approach to error handling is important because it means your scripts will be able to deal with unexpected issues and keep the system running smoothly, which is essential in a DevOps environment where continuity is key.

Up and Running with Shell Automation

Shell scripting is a key part of the DevOps toolkit because it's so adaptable and efficient at handling different tasks. The good thing about using shell scripts is that they let DevOps engineers automate repetitive and time-consuming tasks with minimal manual input. This makes them a really useful tool for maintaining fast and reliable CI/CD processes. Shell scripting is great for managing deployments, monitoring server health, and adjusting configurations. It bridges the gap between operations and development, enabling seamless integration and faster issue resolution. Plus, shell scripts require fewer resources than full-fledged programming languages, making them lightweight yet powerful enough to handle a range of DevOps tasks efficiently. By minimizing human error and standardizing processes, shell scripting strengthens system reliability and helps maintain a consistent environment across different stages of deployment.

Starting with shell scripting, DevOps teams typically work in a Unix or Linux environment, with Bash being the most commonly used shell. However, some systems use the C shell (**csh**), which has slightly different syntax and commands but can serve as a helpful alternative in specific scenarios.

To begin with, first, ensure that you have access to the C shell by running the following command in your terminal to confirm its presence:

```
which csh
```

If the output provides a path to **csh**, the shell is installed. If not, you can install it using your package manager, for example, by running:

```
sudo apt install csh
```

Although Bash remains the preferred scripting language in most DevOps scenarios, understanding and configuring alternatives like the C shell can add flexibility when working across different systems. Once the C shell is set up, switching back to Bash for scripting is straightforward.

Now, to confirm the Bash shell version, use:

```
bash --version
```

The command confirms you are using the desired shell and provides version details, which can be useful for compatibility checks.

Getting Started with Bash Scripting

We will now dive into Bash scripting. Start by opening a text editor of your choice, such as Vim, Nano, or any IDE, and create a new script file. Save it with a **.sh** extension (for example, **my_first_script.sh**) to indicate it's a shell script. To get started with Bash scripts, you'll want to include a "shebang" line at the beginning. This is basically your interpreter command, which tells the script what to run.

Here's what the shebang line looks like for Bash scripts:

```
#!/bin/bash
```

The shebang line tells the system to use the Bash shell to interpret the script, which makes it compatible when you run it on different systems. After the shebang, you can write a simple command. For this first script, we're going to automate a basic task: displaying system information like the current date, system uptime, and user count.

Following is the code:

```
#!/bin/bash
# Display current date and time
echo "Current Date and Time: $(date)"
# Display system uptime
echo "System Uptime: $(uptime -p)"
# Display the number of users currently logged in
```

```
echo "Number of Users Logged In: $(who | wc -l)"
```

Next, save this script and exit the editor. Before running it, ensure the script is executable. This can be achieved by modifying its permissions using the **chmod** command:

```
chmod +x my_first_script.sh
```

This command makes the script executable by the current user. To execute the script, use the following command:

```
./my_first_script.sh
```

You should see a display showing the current date, how long the system has been up, and the number of users currently logged in. The point of this simple script is to show just how simple it is to automate information retrieval in a DevOps environment.

Now, the script you just created utilizes a few key elements common in Bash automation:

- **Commands with Flags**: The **date**, **uptime**, and **who** commands retrieve system information, while the **wc -l** command counts lines. Using commands with specific flags allows you to customize the output according to your needs.
- **Variable Substitution**: The **$(command)** syntax, known as command substitution, allows you to embed the output of one command within another. For example, **$(date)** inserts the current date and time directly into the echo statement, streamlining the process.
- **Echo Statements**: Echo statements display information to the user. This command is essential for providing output or logging information in more advanced scripts.

Add Flexibility Parameters

To increase the utility of shell scripts, you can add parameters that allow users to specify options when running the script. For instance, let's say you want to add an option that only shows detailed system info when you ask for it. For this, following is what you need to do to the script:

```
#!/bin/bash
# Check if the "detailed" parameter is provided
if [[ $1 == "detailed" ]]; then
    # Display detailed system information
    echo "Detailed System Information:"
    echo "-----------------------------------"
```

```
    echo "System Name: $(uname -n)"
    echo "Kernel Version: $(uname -r)"
    echo "Memory Usage: $(free -h)"
    echo "Disk Usage: $(df -h /)"
    echo "Processes Running: $(ps aux | wc -l)"
else
    # Display basic information
    echo "Current Date and Time: $(date)"
    echo "System Uptime: $(uptime -p)"
    echo "Number of Users Logged In: $(who | wc -l)"
fi
```

The script checks whether the parameter "detailed" is passed. If it is, the script outputs additional information, including kernel version, memory usage, disk usage, and the count of active processes. To run this version with the parameter, enter:

```
./my_first_script.sh detailed
```

Run Scripts on Schedule

In DevOps, it's common to automate tasks that need to run at specific intervals. You can schedule scripts using **crontab**, which allows users to set up periodic execution of commands. Now, here we will schedule the basic script to run every hour and log its output to a file.

Open the crontab editor:

```
crontab -e
```

Add the following line to run the script every hour and log the output:

```
0 * * * * /path/to/my_first_script.sh >> /path/to/logfile.log
```

This above line tells the system to execute the script at the start of every hour. The **>>** operator appends the output to a log file, allowing you to track historical data over time.

Bash Variables for Enhanced Customization

If you want to add more customization, you can introduce variables in your scripts. With variables, you can save values that you can reuse throughout the script, which makes things more efficient and easier to update. Take a look below at this revised script that uses variables to save command results before displaying them:

```
#!/bin/bash
# Define variables
current_time=$(date)
system_uptime=$(uptime -p)
user_count=$(who | wc -l)
# Display information
echo "Current Date and Time: $current_time"
echo "System Uptime: $system_uptime"
echo "Number of Users Logged In: $user_count"
```

Variables streamline the script, allowing changes to be made quickly by updating the variable definitions at the beginning. Additionally, variables can be passed between functions or used to hold output values for processing in more complex scripts.

Creating Reusable Scripts

Reusable scripts are a great way to make DevOps tasks more efficient. They let you create versatile code that can be adapted for different situations, so you don't have to rewrite new scripts every time. This gives you more efficiency, and it's easy to modify or extend functionality as your DevOps environment changes. Rather than having one script for each task, reusable scripts are designed to be used again and again. They have modules with functions and parameters that can be used to perform different operations within one script.

Build Modular Script with Functions

To start creating reusable scripts, consider using functions, which allow specific pieces of code to execute independently. Functions help organize code by encapsulating each task, reducing redundancy and making troubleshooting easier. So here, we will begin by creating a script that checks for system updates, retrieves disk space usage, and monitors user activity, all within one modular script.

To do this, first, create a new file called **modular_script.sh** and start with the shebang line to indicate the script interpreter:

```
#!/bin/bash
```

Next, define separate functions to handle each task. What I mean is, one function can handle system updates, another can manage disk space checks, and a third can monitor active users. By organizing each task within its function, the script becomes more readable and easier to maintain.

```
#!/bin/bash
# Function to check for system updates
check_updates() {
    echo "Checking for system updates..."
    sudo apt update > /dev/null 2>&1
    if [[ $? -eq 0 ]]; then
        echo "System updates are available."
    else
        echo "Failed to check for updates."
    fi
}
# Function to check disk space usage
check_disk_space() {
    echo "Checking disk space usage..."
    disk_usage=$(df -h / | grep '/' | awk '{print $5}')
    echo "Disk usage for root partition: $disk_usage"
}
# Function to count active users
check_active_users() {
    echo "Checking active users..."
    user_count=$(who | wc -l)
    echo "Number of users currently logged in: $user_count"
}
```

Each function performs a specific task, and the use of **echo** statements helps keep track of the progress within each function. The script above now has a modular structure, making each section easy to modify independently.

Run Multiple Tasks in One Execution

To further enhance the script, we can allow the user to specify multiple tasks to execute at once. By adding a loop, the script can iterate over the parameters and execute each corresponding function as needed. To do this, modify the **modular_script.sh** as shown below:

```
#!/bin/bash
# Function to check for system updates
check_updates() {
    echo "Checking for system updates..."
    sudo apt update > /dev/null 2>&1
    if [[ $? -eq 0 ]]; then
        echo "System updates are available."
    else
        echo "Failed to check for updates."
    fi
}
# Function to check disk space usage
check_disk_space() {
    echo "Checking disk space usage..."
    disk_usage=$(df -h / | grep '/' | awk '{print $5}')
    echo "Disk usage for root partition: $disk_usage"
}
# Function to count active users
check_active_users() {
    echo "Checking active users..."
    user_count=$(who | wc -l)
    echo "Number of users currently logged in: $user_count"
}
# Loop through each provided argument
```

```
for task in "$@"; do
    case $task in
        updates)
            check_updates
            ;;
        disk)
            check_disk_space
            ;;
        users)
            check_active_users
            ;;
        *)
            echo "Unknown task: $task"
            echo "Usage: $0 {updates|disk|users}"
            ;;
    esac
done
```

Now here, the script can handle multiple tasks in a single run.

Add Optional Logging

Sometimes it can be helpful to keep a record of the output for future reference or to do some more in-depth analysis. If you want to log your output, you can just add an optional feature that lets you specify where you want the output to go. Just update the script to check if a log file is specified as an additional argument. If it is, redirect the output to that file.

To do this, modify the **modular_script.sh** as follows:

```
#!/bin/bash
# Function to check for system updates
check_updates() {
    echo "Checking for system updates..."
    sudo apt update > /dev/null 2>&1
```

```
    if [[ $? -eq 0 ]]; then
        echo "System updates are available."
    else
        echo "Failed to check for updates."
    fi
}
# Function to check disk space usage
check_disk_space() {
    echo "Checking disk space usage..."
    disk_usage=$(df -h / | grep '/' | awk '{print $5}')
    echo "Disk usage for root partition: $disk_usage"
}
# Function to count active users
check_active_users() {
    echo "Checking active users..."
    user_count=$(who | wc -l)
    echo "Number of users currently logged in: $user_count"
}
# Check if log file is provided
if [[ $1 == "--log" ]]; then
    log_file=$2
    shift 2
fi
# Execute tasks and log if specified
for task in "$@"; do
    {
        case $task in
            updates)
                check_updates
```

```
                ;;
            disk)
                check_disk_space
                ;;
            users)
                check_active_users
                ;;
            *)
                echo "Unknown task: $task"
                echo "Usage: $0 [--log logfile]
{updates|disk|users}"
                ;;
        esac
    } | tee -a "$log_file"
done
```

Here now, the script supports a logging option. If we run **./modular_script.sh --log system_report.log updates disk**, it will output results to the console and append the results to **system_report.log**.

All these elements collectively form a robust and scalable approach to shell scripting, making it easy to adjust the script according to specific needs without repetitive rewrites.

Error Handling and Logging

It's super important to get error handling right in shell scripting, particularly in DevOps, where scripts automate key tasks across a range of different systems. Errors can pop up from all sorts of places, like if you use the wrong command, have the wrong file permissions, get unexpected input, or even just make a simple mistake in the syntax. If you can spot these common errors and put some simple error-handling techniques in place, you can stop scripts from failing out of the blue. Logging mechanisms are also great for recording what's going on and any errors that might come up. That way, you can quickly figure out what's wrong when something goes wrong. Once you know about these common mistakes, you can make your scripts more solid and reliable from the start.

A few common mistakes people make when writing shell scripts:

1. **Command Not Found**: Often caused by typing mistakes, missing commands, or the absence of required packages.
2. **Permission Denied**: Occurs when scripts attempt to access files or directories without appropriate permissions, especially when modifying system files.
3. **Unexpected User Input**: When a script expects specific input but receives something else, it can cause the script to behave unpredictably or fail.
4. **File or Directory Not Found**: Scripts often interact with files or directories that may not exist, causing commands to fail if they rely on such files.

Below are several scenarios that demonstrate these above types of errors and ways to handle them to make scripts more dependable.

Scenario 1: Handle Command Not Found Errors

A common issue in shell scripting is the "command not found" error, which usually arises when the script tries to execute a command that doesn't exist on the system. This can happen if a required package isn't installed or if there's a typo in the command.

Let us consider a script that uses **curl** to fetch data from a URL. If **curl** isn't installed, the script will throw an error:

```
#!/bin/bash

# Attempt to fetch data from a URL

curl http://example.com/data
```

To handle this, you can add a check to ensure **curl** is installed before running the command:

```
#!/bin/bash

# Check if curl is installed

if ! command -v curl &> /dev/null; then

    echo "Error: curl is not installed. Please install it and
try again."

    exit 1

fi

# Attempt to fetch data from a URL

curl http://example.com/data
```

This approach uses **command -v** to check for the presence of **curl**. If it's missing, the script prints an error message and exits with a non-zero status (**exit 1**), signaling that it didn't complete successfully. This technique is applicable for any command that may not be available on all systems, helping prevent errors from breaking the script unexpectedly.

Scenario 2: Handle Permission Denied Errors

If you get an error message saying you don't have permission to access a file or directory, it's probably because the script trying to access it doesn't have the necessary permissions. For instance, you might need root privileges if you're trying to create or modify files in a system directory.

Consider a script that writes to **/var/log/custom.log**, a location where root privileges are typically required:

```
#!/bin/bash
# Attempt to write to a log file
echo "Log entry" >> /var/log/custom.log
```

If you don't have the required permissions, this will trigger a "Permission denied" error. So to handle this, you can check the permissions on the target directory before attempting to write, and inform the user if root access is needed.

```
#!/bin/bash
# Check if script has permission to write to /var/log
if [[ ! -w /var/log ]]; then
    echo "Error: Permission denied. Please run as root or use sudo."
    exit 1
fi
# Write to the log file
echo "Log entry" >> /var/log/custom.log
```

This script checks if the user has write access to **/var/log**. If not, it displays an error message and exits. This check prevents the script from failing due to permission issues and provides clear guidance on how to fix the problem.

Scenario 3: Handle Missing/Non-Existent files

A lot of scripts depend on certain files or directories being there, but if they're not, it can cause problems. For example, a script might try to read from a configuration file that doesn't exist, which would make commands fail.

Let us consider the following script, which reads configuration settings from **config.txt**:

```
#!/bin/bash
# Read configuration file
config=$(cat config.txt)
echo "Configuration: $config"
```

If **config.txt** doesn't exist, the script will return an error. To avoid this, add a check to verify the file's existence before reading it:

```
#!/bin/bash
# Check if config.txt exists
if [[ ! -f config.txt ]]; then
    echo "Error: config.txt not found."
    exit 1
fi
# Read configuration file
config=$(cat config.txt)
echo "Configuration: $config"
```

Using the **-f** flag, this check confirms the presence of **config.txt**. If the file is missing, the script displays an error and exits. This prevents the script from failing due to a missing file and provides a clear message about the issue.

Scenario 4: Handle Unexpected Input

When scripts receive input from users or other systems, unexpected data can cause them to behave unpredictably. For instance, a script that calculates disk usage might expect the user to enter a directory path. If the user enters an invalid path, the command may fail.

Here is an example where the script expects a directory as input:

```
#!/bin/bash
# Expect directory as input
echo "Enter directory to check disk usage:"
read dir
```

```
# Check disk usage of directory
du -sh "$dir"
```

If the user enters a non-existent directory, the script will fail. You can add a check to confirm the directory exists before proceeding:

```
#!/bin/bash
# Expect directory as input
echo "Enter directory to check disk usage:"
read dir
# Check if directory exists
if [[ ! -d "$dir" ]]; then
    echo "Error: Directory does not exist."
    exit 1
fi
# Check disk usage of directory
du -sh "$dir"
```

The **-d** flag verifies that the specified path is a directory. If the directory doesn't exist, the script prints an error and exits. This approach prevents unexpected input from causing the script to fail and provides feedback to the user about the required input format.

If you put these error checks in your scripts, you'll make sure they can handle unexpected situations without any hiccups. And users won't get left in the lurch with no information when something goes wrong. They'll just get a heads up that there's an issue and you'll be able to work it out quickly.

Knowledge Exercise

I've put together a set of 10 questions with multiple-choice answers to help you remember what you learned in this chapter. Each question builds on topics we've covered so far, gradually reinforcing concepts around automation, reusable scripts, error handling, and logging.

Question 1: What is a key benefit of using shell scripting for routine DevOps tasks?

A. It replaces all manual intervention permanently.

B. It improves workflow efficiency by automating repetitive tasks.

C. It avoids the need for any error handling.

D. It provides detailed debugging information by default.

Answer: **B**. Shell scripting automates repetitive tasks, thus improving workflow efficiency, which is essential where consistency is critical.

Question 2: What does the shebang line (`#!/bin/bash`) in a shell script accomplish?

A. It specifies the script should be run with root permissions.

B. It signals to the system that Bash should interpret the script.

C. It specifies the default path for script execution.

D. It automatically runs the script without further permission settings.

Answer: **B**. The shebang (**`#!/bin/bash`**) tells the system to use Bash as the interpreter, ensuring compatibility across systems where multiple shell environments may be present.

Question 3: In the context of reusable scripts, what is the primary advantage of using functions?

A. Functions eliminate the need for error handling.

B. Functions ensure that every script is modular and single-use only.

C. Functions allow specific tasks to be organized and reused across multiple parts of a script.

D. Functions execute without requiring arguments or parameters.

Answer: **C**. Functions enable modularity within scripts, organizing tasks into reusable blocks that can be executed as needed, enhancing the flexibility and reusability of the script.

Question 4: Given the script below, what will be the output if `check_updates` is called but `curl` is not installed on the system?

```
check_updates() {
    if ! command -v curl &> /dev/null; then
        echo "Error: curl is not installed."
        exit 1
    fi
    curl http://example.com/data
```

```
}
```

A. The script will fetch data from **`example.com`** without issue.

B. The script will display "Error: curl is not installed" and then terminate.

C. The script will display no output at all and continue running.

D. The script will throw a "Permission Denied" error.

Answer: **B**. If **`curl`** is missing, the script's check will print "Error: curl is not installed" and exit, demonstrating the use of error checking before executing a command.

Question 5: How does parameter handling improve the flexibility of a script?

A. It allows a script to adapt based on different inputs provided during execution.

B. It restricts the script to a single task and reduces usability.

C. It increases script complexity without functional advantages.

D. It guarantees that all system commands will succeed without errors.

Answer: Parameter handling makes scripts adaptable, allowing specific tasks to run based on input, making scripts more flexible and reducing the need to rewrite them for each variation.

Question 6: In a script that logs activities, why is it beneficial to include timestamps in the log entries?

A. Timestamps enable more efficient execution of commands.

B. Timestamps prevent errors from occurring during script execution.

C. Timestamps provide context on when each action occurred, aiding in troubleshooting.

D. Timestamps eliminate the need for error handling.

Answer: **C**. Including timestamps in logs helps track when actions occurred, which is valuable for diagnosing issues and reviewing the sequence of events in scripts.

Question 7: Consider the following scenario. What does the script below output if `config.txt` is missing?

```
if [[ ! -f config.txt ]]; then
    echo "Error: config.txt not found."
```

```
    exit 1
fi
cat config.txt
```

A. The script continues to read **config.txt** without issue.

B. The script throws a "Permission Denied" error.

C. The script outputs "Error: config.txt not found" and terminates.

D. The script outputs an empty line and then exits.

Answer: **C**. If **config.txt** is missing, the script checks for its existence and, finding it absent, prints an error message and exits before attempting to read the file.

Question 8: What would happen if a user specifies a non-existent directory as input in the following script?

```
echo "Enter directory to check disk usage:"
read dir
if [[ ! -d "$dir" ]]; then
    echo "Error: Directory does not exist."
    exit 1
fi
du -sh "$dir"
```

A. The script continues without errors, even if the directory doesn't exist.

B. The script outputs "Error: Directory does not exist" and terminates if the directory is missing.

C. The script ignores any errors and checks disk usage regardless.

D. The script throws a "Command Not Found" error.

Answer: **B**. The script checks if the specified directory exists and, if not, outputs an error message and exits, demonstrating the handling of missing input.

Question 9: What purpose does `chmod +x script.sh` serve when working with shell scripts?

A. It compiles the script, making it faster.

B. It changes the file extension to **`.x`**, a format recognized by the system.

C. It makes the script executable, allowing it to be run directly.

D. It sets the script to run as root.

Answer: **C**. The command **`chmod +x`** makes the script executable by the user, allowing them to run it directly without calling it via an interpreter.

Question 10: When using the `tee` command to log both console output and write to a log file, what does the `-a` flag do?

A. It overwrites the log file each time the script runs.

B. It appends the output to the existing log file without overwriting it.

C. It archives the log file to another directory.

D. It enables automatic error correction in the log file.

Answer: **B**. The **`-a`** flag appends output to the existing log file, preventing it from being overwritten, which is useful for maintaining a continuous log across multiple script executions.

CHAPTER 2: MANAGING CI/CD PIPELINES WITH SHELL SCRIPTING

Overview

In this chapter, we're going to look at how to use Bash scripting to make your CI/CD pipelines more automated in DevOps workflows. We will take a look at how you can automate different parts of the CI/CD pipeline, including building, testing, and deploying applications. When you automate these steps, you reduce the number of manual interventions and ensure that everything is executed in the same way in different environments, making processes more efficient and reliable.

Next, we will look at how to connect Bash scripts with popular CI/CD tools, including Jenkins and GitLab CI. This integration lets you interact with these platforms programmatically, which gives you more control and flexibility in managing pipeline jobs. When you connect Jenkins and GitLab CI, you make it easy to automate everything in a really smooth, coordinated way.

Finally, we will look at how to create scripts that handle code rollbacks and redeployments efficiently. If you automate these important processes, you will have less downtime and be able to fix any deployment issues more quickly. This makes your system more reliable overall.

Automating CI/CD Pipeline Steps

I'd say that CI/CD are pretty much essential for modern DevOps practices. CI automatically builds and tests code every time a team member makes a change, so the codebase stays stable. CD takes it a step further by automatically deploying code changes to production or staging environments, which makes it easier to roll out new features and fix any bugs quickly. I've found that automating these steps helps to cut down on manual input, avoid mistakes, and speed up the whole development process.

To show you how to automate CI/CD pipeline steps using Bash scripting, we'll look at a sample project: a simple web application written in Node.js. The idea is to create a script that will automate the build, test, and deployment processes, and then integrate them into one automated pipeline.

Setting up Project Structure

Let us consider that we have a Node.js application with the below structure:

```
myapp/
    ├── app.js
    ├── package.json
    ├── tests/
        └── test_app.js
```

The application code resides in **app.js**, dependencies are listed in **package.json**, and tests are located in the **tests/** directory.

Create the Build Script

The build step involves installing dependencies and preparing the application for deployment. So let us create a script named **build.sh**:

```
#!/bin/bash
echo "Starting build process..."
# Install dependencies
npm install
# Check if npm install was successful
if [[ $? -ne 0 ]]; then
    echo "Build failed: npm install encountered an error."
    exit 1
fi
echo "Build completed successfully."
```

This script installs the necessary packages using **npm install** and checks if the command was successful by examining the exit status (**$?**). If the installation fails, the script outputs an error message and exits with a non-zero status.

```
Now next is to chmod +x build.sh
```

Create Test Script

The good thing about automated testing is that it makes sure that new code changes don't break anything that's already working. So let us create a script named **test.sh**:

```
#!/bin/bash
echo "Starting test process..."
# Run tests
npm test
# Check if tests passed
if [[ $? -ne 0 ]]; then
```

```
    echo "Tests failed."
    exit 1
fi
echo "All tests passed successfully."
```

Assuming that **npm test** is configured to run your test suite, this script then executes the tests and checks for success. If tests fail, it prints an error message and exits.

Then, make the script executable as below:

```
chmod +x test.sh
```

Create Deployment Script

In a nutshell, deployment is moving the built-up app to a testing or live environment. So next, you need to create a script named **deploy.sh**:

```
#!/bin/bash
echo "Starting deployment process..."
# Define deployment server and directory
DEPLOY_SERVER="user@gitforgits.com"
DEPLOY_DIR="/var/www/myapp"
# Archive the application files
tar -czf myapp.tar.gz app.js package.json node_modules
# Transfer files to the deployment server
scp myapp.tar.gz $DEPLOY_SERVER:/tmp/
# Check if scp was successful
if [[ $? -ne 0 ]]; then
    echo "Deployment failed: File transfer error."
    exit 1
fi
# Connect to the server and deploy
ssh $DEPLOY_SERVER << 'ENDSSH'
tar -xzf /tmp/myapp.tar.gz -C $DEPLOY_DIR
```

```
rm /tmp/myapp.tar.gz
cd $DEPLOY_DIR
npm install --production
pm2 restart all
ENDSSH
echo "Deployment completed successfully."
```

This script performs the following actions:

- Archives the application files into **myapp.tar.gz**.
- Transfers the archive to the deployment server using **scp**.
- Connects to the deployment server via **ssh** and:
    - Extracts the archive into the deployment directory.
    - Removes the temporary archive file.
    - Installs production dependencies.
    - Restarts the application using **pm2** (a process manager for Node.js).

Now here, make sure you replace **user@gitforgits.com** and **/var/www/myapp** with your actual server credentials and deployment path. Also, ensure that SSH keys are set up for passwordless authentication to automate the process fully.

```
chmod +x deploy.sh
```

Create CI/CD Pipeline Script

Let us now create a master script that orchestrates the build, test, and deploy steps. And we shall name it **pipeline.sh**:

```
#!/bin/bash
echo "Starting CI/CD pipeline..."
# Run build script
./build.sh
if [[ $? -ne 0 ]]; then
    echo "CI/CD pipeline failed at build stage."
    exit 1
```

```
fi
# Run test script
./test.sh
if [[ $? -ne 0 ]]; then
    echo "CI/CD pipeline failed at test stage."
    exit 1
fi
# Run deployment script
./deploy.sh
if [[ $? -ne 0 ]]; then
    echo "CI/CD pipeline failed at deployment stage."
    exit 1
fi
echo "CI/CD pipeline completed successfully."
```

This above script sequentially runs the build, test, and deployment scripts, checking the exit status after each step. If any step fails, it exits the pipeline with an appropriate message.

Execute CI/CD Pipeline

To run the entire pipeline, execute:

```
./pipeline.sh
```

This is where you'll see how things are going with each stage. By making these steps automated, you can be sure that code changes are built, tested, and deployed consistently and without any manual input.

Integrating with Jenkins and GitLab CI

Jenkins is a widely used automation server that can orchestrate your CI/CD pipelines. If you combine your Bash scripts with tools like Jenkins and GitLab CI, you can make the most of their awesome features for scheduling, logging, and monitoring pipeline runs.

Integrate with Jenkins

Setting up a Jenkins Job

Assuming Jenkins is already installed and running on your server. We then following following steps:

- Create a New Job:
    - Navigate to Jenkins Dashboard.
    - Click on **"New Item"**.
    - Enter a job name, e.g., **`MyApp_CI_CD_Pipeline`**.
    - Select **"Freestyle project"** and click **"OK"**.
- Configure the Job:
    - Source Code Management:
        - Select **"Git"**.
        - Enter your repository URL.
    - Build Triggers:
        - Check **"Poll SCM"** if you want Jenkins to check for changes periodically.
        - Set the schedule, e.g., **`H/5 * * * *`** to poll every 5 minutes.
    - Build Environment:
        - Add any environment variables if necessary.
    - Build Steps:
        - **Add build step**: Select **"Execute shell"**.

Then, enter the following command to run your pipeline script:

```
./pipeline.sh
```

Now here, ensure that your scripts are executable and located in the repository.

- **Save** the configuration.

Executing Jenkins Job

- Click **"Build Now"** to manually trigger the job.
- Jenkins will execute **`pipeline.sh`**, and you can monitor the progress in the console output.

Handling Credentials and Permissions

- Just make sure the Jenkins user has the right SSH keys for accessing the Git repository and logging into the deployment server.
- The Jenkins user should have the ability to run the scripts and perform deployment actions.

Integrate with GitLab CI

GitLab CI/CD is integrated into GitLab repositories and uses a YAML file to define the pipeline.

Creating **`gitlab-ci.yml`** *file*

At the root of your repository, create a file named **`gitlab-ci.yml`**:

```
stages:
  - build
  - test
  - deploy
build_job:
  stage: build
  script:
    - ./build.sh
  only:
    - master
test_job:
  stage: test
  script:
    - ./test.sh
  only:
    - master
deploy_job:
  stage: deploy
  script:
```

```
    - ./deploy.sh
  only:
    - master
```

This configuration defines three stages: **build**, **test**, and **deploy**. Each job runs the corresponding script. The **only** keyword ensures that the pipeline runs only on the **master** branch.

Setting up Runners

GitLab CI requires runners to execute the jobs. To make use of them, first:

- Register a Runner:
  - Install GitLab Runner on your server.
  - Register the runner using the registration token from your GitLab project.
- Configure the Runner:
  - Ensure the runner has access to necessary environment variables and permissions.
  - If deploying to remote servers, make sure SSH keys are configured.

Using Environment Variables

You can store sensitive information, like server credentials, in GitLab CI variables.

- Navigate to **"Settings"** > **"CI/CD"** > **"Variables"** in your GitLab project.
- Add variables such as **DEPLOY_SERVER** and **DEPLOY_DIR**.

And then modify your scripts to use these variables:

```
DEPLOY_SERVER="$DEPLOY_SERVER"
DEPLOY_DIR="$DEPLOY_DIR"
```

Interact with CI/CD Tool APIs

Both Jenkins and GitLab CI offer APIs to interact programmatically. You can include API calls in your scripts to perform actions like triggering jobs or updating build statuses.

For example, to trigger a Jenkins job from a script:

```
#!/bin/bash
```

```
JENKINS_URL="http://jenkins-server"
JOB_NAME="MyApp_CI_CD_Pipeline"
API_TOKEN="YOUR_API_TOKEN"
USER="your_username"
# Trigger Jenkins job
curl -X POST "$JENKINS_URL/job/$JOB_NAME/build" \
  --user "$USER:$API_TOKEN"
```

Monitor Pipeline Status

You can automate the monitoring of pipeline status by querying the CI/CD tool's API.

For instance, here's how you can check the status of a GitLab pipeline:

```
#!/bin/bash
PROJECT_ID="YOUR_PROJECT_ID"
PIPELINE_ID="YOUR_PIPELINE_ID"
PRIVATE_TOKEN="YOUR_PRIVATE_TOKEN"
# Get pipeline status
status=$(curl --header "PRIVATE-TOKEN: $PRIVATE_TOKEN" \

"https://gitlab.com/api/v4/projects/$PROJECT_ID/pipelines/$PIP
ELINE_ID" \
  | jq -r '.status')
echo "Pipeline status: $status"
```

This script uses **curl** to fetch the pipeline status and **jq** to parse the JSON response. Ensure **jq** is installed on your system.

Scripted Code Rollbacks and Redeployments

No matter what your deployment workflow looks like, it's really important to be able to roll back changes quickly if you want to keep your system stable. As with any new software, there are bound to be a few unexpected issues after deployment, such as bugs, performance drops, or compatibility problems. If you automate rollbacks, you can easily get back to a stable point in your system without any downtime, which is great for your apps. In this section, we'll look at ways to automate rollbacks and redeployments for our Node.js project, and add these features to our current CI/CD pipeline.

Implement Version Control with Git Tags

To facilitate rollbacks, it's important to have version control in place. Using Git tags allows you to mark specific commits as release points, making it easy to reference and deploy stable versions. So let us begin by tagging stable releases in your repository:

```
git tag -a v1.0 -m "Stable release v1.0"
git push origin v1.0
```

Here, by annotating releases, you create clear checkpoints to which you can return if necessary. This practice is crucial for consistent rollbacks and redeployments.

Enhance Deployment Script

Just tweak the **deploy.sh** script to accept a version parameter, and you can deploy specific tagged versions. This change lets you deploy and roll back to any version you want.

```
#!/bin/bash
echo "Starting deployment process..."
# Define variables
DEPLOY_SERVER="user@gitforgits.com"
DEPLOY_DIR="/var/www/myapp"
VERSION_TAG=$1
if [[ -z "$VERSION_TAG" ]]; then
    echo "Usage: ./deploy.sh <version_tag>"
    exit 1
fi
# SSH into the deployment server
ssh $DEPLOY_SERVER << EOF
    cd $DEPLOY_DIR
    git fetch --all
    git checkout $VERSION_TAG
```

```
    npm install --production
    pm2 restart all
EOF
if [[ $? -ne 0 ]]; then
    echo "Deployment failed."
    exit 1
fi
echo "Deployment of version $VERSION_TAG completed
successfully."
```

This script checks out the specified Git tag on the deployment server, ensuring that the exact version is deployed.

Create Rollback Script

Let's put together a **rollback.sh** script that can automate the process of reverting to a previous stable version. This script makes it easier to roll back, so it's more consistent and less likely to have errors.

```
#!/bin/bash
echo "Starting rollback process..."
# Define variables
DEPLOY_SERVER="user@gitforgits.com"
DEPLOY_DIR="/var/www/myapp"
PREV_VERSION_TAG=$1
if [[ -z "$PREV_VERSION_TAG" ]]; then
    echo "Usage: ./rollback.sh <previous_version_tag>"
    exit 1
fi
# SSH into the deployment server
ssh $DEPLOY_SERVER << EOF
    cd $DEPLOY_DIR
    git fetch --all
```

```
    git checkout $PREV_VERSION_TAG
    npm install --production
    pm2 restart all
EOF
if [[ $? -ne 0 ]]; then
    echo "Rollback failed."
    exit 1
fi
echo "Rollback to version $PREV_VERSION_TAG completed
successfully."
```

This script basically copies the deployment process but uses an older version. If you automate rollbacks, you can save time and effort when you need to get your service up and running smoothly again.

Integrate Rollback Logic into Pipeline

We need to update the **pipeline.sh** script and add a rollback logic section. If you can spot when a deployment fails and automatically roll back, you'll make your CI/CD pipeline more robust.

```
#!/bin/bash
echo "Starting CI/CD pipeline..."
# Set the version tag
VERSION_TAG="v1.1"
# Run build script
./build.sh
if [[ $? -ne 0 ]]; then
    echo "Build failed."
    exit 1
fi
# Run test script
./test.sh
```

```
if [[ $? -ne 0 ]]; then
    echo "Tests failed."
    exit 1
fi
# Run deployment script
./deploy.sh $VERSION_TAG
if [[ $? -ne 0 ]]; then
    echo "Deployment failed. Initiating rollback..."
    ./rollback.sh "v1.0"
    exit 1
fi
echo "CI/CD pipeline completed successfully."
```

Here, by specifying both the deployment and rollback versions, you maintain clarity over which versions are active. The pipeline now automatically rolls back if deployment issues occur, minimizing downtime.

Handle Configuration and Database Changes

These above rollbacks can become complex when configuration files or databases change between versions. So, to manage this, we need to:

- Externalize configurations using environment variables or separate configuration management tools. This approach decouples configurations from code, simplifying rollbacks.
- Implement migration scripts that can be rolled back. Tools like **`knex`** or **`sequelize`** provide mechanisms for database version control.

It's important now to test your rollback scripts and make sure they work properly. Testing makes sure your rollback procedures are reliable, so you can feel confident in your automated recovery strategies.

Add Notifications, Logging and Fixing Issues

So here now it is time to incorporate logging and notifications. By informing the team of deployments and rollbacks, you improve transparency and enable swift responses to issues.

```
# Inside rollback.sh
# Send notification
echo "Rollback to version $PREV_VERSION_TAG completed." | mail -s "Rollback Notification" team@example.com
```

Once issues are resolved, redeploy the corrected version:

```
./deploy.sh "v1.2"
```

If you specify the new stable version, you'll make sure the latest fixes are deployed in a systematic way. Therefore, by scripting rollbacks and redeployments, you strengthen your DevOps practices, ensuring that systems remain robust even when challenges arise.

Summary

In a nutshell, we explored ways of managing CI/CD pipelines with Bash scripting to make DevOps workflows more automated. We've automated the CI/CD pipeline steps, which has made our build, test, and deployment processes a lot more efficient. We've also integrated our scripts with tools like Jenkins and GitLab CI. This has let us make the most of their capabilities to manage and keep track of our pipelines.

On top of that, we've also explored the option of rolling back and redeploying scripts when needed. This lets us revert to a stable version pretty quickly if something goes wrong with a deployment. Automating this process means less downtime and a more stable system, which is really important in fast-paced DevOps environments. By adding these scripts into our CI/CD pipeline, we've created a strong and adaptable deployment strategy.

CHAPTER 3: TEST AUTOMATION AND VALIDATION SCRIPTS

Overview

In this chapter, we're going to look at how we can make our software better by automating the testing and validation processes. We will look at how to write automated unit and integration test scripts, so you can create tests that are executed automatically. That way, you can be sure that when code is changed, there are no regressions.

Next, we will look at automating code quality checks, including tasks like static analysis and linting. We will also look at how to make sure everyone's coding follows the same rules and catch any problems early on in the development process. Finally, we will explore how to validate applications and infrastructure after deployment with dynamic scripts. Automating these processes lets you verify your systems are running as they should, which gives you peace of mind when you make a new deployment. This approach quickly flags any issues that need attention.

Writing Automated Unit and Integration Test Scripts

The key to making sure that code changes don't introduce new bugs or regressions is to automate the tests. If you create shell scripts for unit and integration tests, it'll make the testing process much faster and easier to integrate into your development workflow. In our Node.js project, we usually run tests using a testing framework like Mocha or Jest. If you automate these tests with shell scripts, you can make sure they're always executed consistently and easily integrate them into your CI/CD pipelines.

Setting up Testing Framework

Assuming that the project uses Mocha for testing, begin by installing the necessary packages. The **package.json** file should include Mocha as a development dependency:

```
{
  "devDependencies": {
    "mocha": "^8.0.0",
    "chai": "^4.0.0"
  },
  "scripts": {
    "test": "mocha"
  }
```

```
}
```

We need to ensure that the test scripts are located in the **tests/** directory.

Create Test Script

Let us begin to create a shell script named **test.sh** to automate the execution of tests:

```
#!/bin/bash
echo "Starting test process..."
# Run unit tests
echo "Running unit tests..."
npm run test:unit
# Check if unit tests passed
if [[ $? -ne 0 ]]; then
    echo "Unit tests failed."
    exit 1
fi
# Run integration tests
echo "Running integration tests..."
npm run test:integration
# Check if integration tests passed
if [[ $? -ne 0 ]]; then
    echo "Integration tests failed."
    exit 1
fi
echo "All tests passed successfully."
```

This script executes both unit and integration tests, checking the exit status after each to determine success or failure.

Define Test Scripts

It'd be good to update **package.json** to include scripts for unit and integration tests.

```
{
  "scripts": {
    "test": "mocha",
    "test:unit": "mocha tests/unit",
    "test:integration": "mocha tests/integration"
  }
}
```

This setup allows the shell script to run specific types of tests by invoking **npm run test:unit** and **npm run test:integration**.

Then, run the test script:

```
./test.sh
```

The script outputs the progress and results of each test suite. If any tests fail, the script exits with an error message.

Incorporate Environment Variables

Some tests might need certain environment variables. You can edit the script to set these variables:

```
#!/bin/bash
echo "Starting test process..."
# Set environment variables
export NODE_ENV=test
export DB_HOST=localhost
export DB_PORT=5432
# Run unit tests
echo "Running unit tests..."
npm run test:unit
# Check if unit tests passed
if [[ $? -ne 0 ]]; then
    echo "Unit tests failed."
    exit 1
```

```
fi
# Run integration tests
echo "Running integration tests..."
npm run test:integration
# Check if integration tests passed
if [[ $? -ne 0 ]]; then
    echo "Integration tests failed."
    exit 1
fi
echo "All tests passed successfully."
```

By exporting environment variables within the script, you ensure that tests run in the correct context without requiring manual setup.

Generate Test Reports

To make it easier to look over the test results, you can use tools like Mocha's built-in reporters to create reports. Just update the test commands in **`package.json`**.

```
{
  "scripts": {
    "test:unit": "mocha tests/unit --reporter mocha-junit-reporter --reporter-options mochaFile=reports/unit-test-results.xml",
    "test:integration": "mocha tests/integration --reporter mocha-junit-reporter --reporter-options mochaFile=reports/integration-test-results.xml"
  }
}
```

Next, get the **`mocha-junit-reporter`** package installed:

```
npm install --save-dev mocha-junit-reporter
```

Then, modify the test script to handle the reports:

```bash
#!/bin/bash
echo "Starting test process..."
# Clean previous reports
rm -rf reports/
mkdir reports
# Set environment variables
export NODE_ENV=test
export DB_HOST=localhost
export DB_PORT=5432
# Run unit tests
echo "Running unit tests..."
npm run test:unit
if [[ $? -ne 0 ]]; then
    echo "Unit tests failed."
    exit 1
fi
# Run integration tests
echo "Running integration tests..."
npm run test:integration
if [[ $? -ne 0 ]]; then
    echo "Integration tests failed."
    exit 1
fi
echo "All tests passed successfully."
```

The script now generates XML reports in the **reports/** directory, which can be used by CI/CD tools for further processing.

Handle Test Databases

It's often necessary to have a test database for integration tests. It's good to automate the setup and teardown of the test database within the script.

```bash
#!/bin/bash
echo "Starting test process..."
# Set environment variables
export NODE_ENV=test
export DB_HOST=localhost
export DB_PORT=5432
export DB_NAME=test_db
# Create test database
echo "Creating test database..."
psql -U postgres -c "CREATE DATABASE $DB_NAME;"
# Run migrations
echo "Running migrations..."
npm run migrate
# Run integration tests
echo "Running integration tests..."
npm run test:integration
if [[ $? -ne 0 ]]; then
    echo "Integration tests failed."
    # Drop test database
    psql -U postgres -c "DROP DATABASE $DB_NAME;"
    exit 1
fi
# Drop test database
echo "Cleaning up test database..."
psql -U postgres -c "DROP DATABASE $DB_NAME;"
echo "All tests passed successfully."
```

Now, while you do this, you need to ensure that the PostgreSQL command-line tools are available and that the script has the necessary permissions.

Parallelize Tests

Next step is to speed up testing, for which we run the tests in parallel. You can simply modify the test commands using tools like **npm-run-all**:

```
npm install --save-dev npm-run-all
# Update package.json
{
  "scripts": {
    "test:unit": "mocha tests/unit",
    "test:integration": "mocha tests/integration",
    "test:all": "npm-run-all --parallel test:unit
test:integration"
  }
}
```

Then, adjust the test script:

```
#!/bin/bash
echo "Starting parallel test process..."
# Set environment variables
export NODE_ENV=test
# Run all tests in parallel
npm run test:all
if [[ $? -ne 0 ]]; then
    echo "Some tests failed."
    exit 1
fi
echo "All tests passed successfully."
```

The good thing about parallel execution is that it shaves time off the overall testing process, making things more efficient.

Integrate Tests into CI/CD Pipeline

To get the test script into the CI/CD pipeline, just update the **pipeline.sh** file.

```
#!/bin/bash
echo "Starting CI/CD pipeline..."
# Run build script
./build.sh
if [[ $? -ne 0 ]]; then
    echo "Build failed."
    exit 1
fi
# Run test script
./test.sh
if [[ $? -ne 0 ]]; then
    echo "Tests failed."
    exit 1
fi
# Proceed with deployment
./deploy.sh "v1.2"
if [[ $? -ne 0 ]]; then
    echo "Deployment failed."
    exit 1
fi
echo "CI/CD pipeline completed successfully."
```

If you automate tests in the pipeline, you can be sure that only code that passes all tests makes it to deployment.

Automating Code Quality Checks

Keeping the quality of the code high is really important for the success of a project over time. I've found that automating code quality checks like static analysis and linting helps catch potential issues early in the development process. If you add these checks to your workflow, you can make sure everyone's coding follows the same standards and reduce the chance of bugs getting in.

Setting up Linting Tools

Let us start with installing a linting tool like ESLint:

```
npm install --save-dev eslint
```

Next, we initialize the ESLint configuration:

```
npx eslint --init
```

Then, follow the prompts to set up the desired configuration, then choose the style guide and environments relevant to our or any other project you are working upon.

Create Linting Script

We now create a shell script named **`lint.sh`** to automate linting:

```
#!/bin/bash
echo "Starting code linting..."
# Run ESLint
npx eslint .
if [[ $? -ne 0 ]]; then
    echo "Linting errors found."
    exit 1
fi
echo "No linting errors found."
```

This script runs ESLint on all files in the project directory. If any linting errors are found, the script exits with an error.

Configure ESLint Rules

We then customize ESLint rules in the **`.eslintrc.js`** file to match your coding standards. For example:

```
module.exports = {
    "env": {
        "node": true,
        "es2020": true
```

```
    },
    "extends": "eslint:recommended",
    "rules": {
        "no-unused-vars": "warn",
        "no-console": "off",
        "eqeqeq": "error"
    }
};
```

Then we need to adjust the rules to enforce or relax certain coding practices as needed.

Integrate Static Analysis Tools

Static analysis tools like SonarQube or JSHint can be added to catch subtler issues. For simplicity's sake, we'll use JSHint.

```
npm install --save-dev jshint
```

First, create a script named **static_analysis.sh**:

```
#!/bin/bash
echo "Starting static code analysis..."
# Run JSHint
npx jshint .
if [[ $? -ne 0 ]]; then
    echo "Static analysis errors found."
    exit 1
fi
echo "No static analysis errors found."
chmod +x static_analysis.sh
```

Update Test Script with Code Quality Checks

To get this done, modify **test.sh** to include linting and static analysis:

```bash
#!/bin/bash
echo "Starting test and code quality checks..."
# Run linting
./lint.sh
if [[ $? -ne 0 ]]; then
    echo "Linting failed."
    exit 1
fi
# Run static analysis
./static_analysis.sh
if [[ $? -ne 0 ]]; then
    echo "Static analysis failed."
    exit 1
fi
# Run unit tests
npm run test:unit
if [[ $? -ne 0 ]]; then
    echo "Unit tests failed."
    exit 1
fi
# Run integration tests
npm run test:integration
if [[ $? -ne 0 ]]; then
    echo "Integration tests failed."
    exit 1
fi
echo "All tests and code quality checks passed successfully."
```

Generate Code Quality Reports

Next, configure ESLint and JSHint to generate reports. For ESLint, use the **--format** option:

```
npx eslint . -f html -o reports/eslint-report.html
```

Then, update the **lint.sh**:

```
#!/bin/bash
echo "Starting code linting..."
# Create reports directory
mkdir -p reports
# Run ESLint with HTML report
npx eslint . -f html -o reports/eslint-report.html
if [[ $? -ne 0 ]]; then
    echo "Linting errors found."
    exit 1
fi
echo "No linting errors found."
```

For JSHint, use the **--reporter** option:

```
npx jshint . --reporter=jslint > reports/jshint-report.xml
```

Then, update **static_analysis.sh** accordingly.

Integrate Code Quality Checks into the CI/CD Pipeline

Modify **pipeline.sh** to include the updated test script:

```
#!/bin/bash
echo "Starting CI/CD pipeline..."
# Run build script
./build.sh
if [[ $? -ne 0 ]]; then
    echo "Build failed."
    exit 1
```

```
fi
# Run test script (includes code quality checks)
./test.sh
if [[ $? -ne 0 ]]; then
    echo "Tests or code quality checks failed."
    exit 1
fi
# Proceed with deployment
./deploy.sh "v1.2"
if [[ $? -ne 0 ]]; then
    echo "Deployment failed."
    exit 1
fi
echo "CI/CD pipeline completed successfully."
```

Automate Code Formatting

There are lots of tools out there that can help you automate your code formatting, such as Prettier.

```
npm install --save-dev prettier
# Create a script named format.sh
#!/bin/bash
echo "Formatting code..."
npx prettier --write .
echo "Code formatting completed."
```

Then, run the above script before linting to ensure code adheres to formatting standards.

Enforce Commit Standards with Husky

We caln also take assistance of Husky to enforce pre-commit hooks that run linting and tests:

```
npm install --save-dev husky
```

```
# Enable Git hooks
npx husky install
# Add a pre-commit hook
npx husky add .husky/pre-commit "npm run lint && npm test"
```

This setup ensures that code cannot be committed unless it passes linting and tests.

Dynamic Validation with Shell Scripts

I'll show you how to automate the validation process with shell scripts so you can be sure your systems are performing well and reliable. So here, in this section, we'll create scripts to validate our Node.js project, focusing on application health, endpoint responsiveness, and infrastructure integrity.

Validate Application Health

First thing's first, we make sure the app is working the way it should by creating a script to check its "health endpoint." Usually, apps have a URL that shows you whether everything's running as it should be.

We first create a script named **health_check.sh**:

```
#!/bin/bash
echo "Starting dynamic validation..."
# Define the health check URL
HEALTH_URL="http://gitforgits.com/health"
# Perform the health check
response=$(curl -s -o /dev/null -w "%{http_code}" $HEALTH_URL)
# Check the HTTP status code
if [[ "$response" -eq 200 ]]; then
    echo "Application is healthy."
else
    echo "Application is unhealthy. HTTP status code:
$response"
    exit 1
```

```
fi
chmod +x health_check.sh
```

This script sends a request to the health endpoint and checks if the HTTP status code is 200 (OK). If the application is unhealthy, it prints an error message and exits with a non-zero status.

Validate API Endpoints

To ensure that critical API endpoints are functioning correctly, extend the script to test specific endpoints.

For this, we modify **health_check.sh**:

```
#!/bin/bash
echo "Starting dynamic validation..."
# Define endpoints to check
ENDPOINTS=(
    "http://gitforgits.com/health"
    "http://gitforgits.com/api/users"
    "http://gitforgits.com/api/orders"
)
# Loop through endpoints
for url in "${ENDPOINTS[@]}"; do
    echo "Checking $url..."
    response=$(curl -s -o /dev/null -w "%{http_code}" $url)
    if [[ "$response" -ne 200 ]]; then
        echo "Error: $url returned status code $response"
        exit 1
    fi
done
echo "All endpoints are responding correctly."
```

This script iterates over a list of endpoints, checking each one for a successful HTTP response. If any endpoint fails, the script exits with an error.

Validate Response Content

Sometimes, it's important to verify not just the status code but also the content of the response. To do this, we update the script to validate response content:

```
#!/bin/bash
echo "Starting dynamic validation..."
# Define endpoint and expected content
ENDPOINT="http://gitforgits.com/api/status"
EXPECTED_CONTENT="\"status\":\"ok\""
# Fetch the response
response=$(curl -s $ENDPOINT)
# Check if response contains expected content
if echo "$response" | grep -q "$EXPECTED_CONTENT"; then
    echo "Endpoint $ENDPOINT is returning expected content."
else
    echo "Error: Unexpected content from $ENDPOINT"
    exit 1
fi
```

This script checks if the response from the **/api/status** endpoint contains the expected JSON content. Adjust the **EXPECTED_CONTENT** variable as needed.

Validate Infrastructure Components

Aside from checking the app, it'd be good to validate your infrastructure components, like your database connections and disk space too. To do this, we create a function within **health_check.sh** to test database connectivity:

```
check_database() {
    echo "Checking database connectivity..."
    PGPASSWORD=$DB_PASSWORD psql -h $DB_HOST -U $DB_USER -d
$DB_NAME -c '\q' 2>/dev/null
    if [[ $? -ne 0 ]]; then
        echo "Error: Unable to connect to the database."
```

```
        exit 1
    else
        echo "Database connectivity is healthy."
    fi
}
# Set database credentials
export DB_HOST="localhost"
export DB_USER="postgres"
export DB_PASSWORD="yourpassword"
export DB_NAME="myapp_db"
# Call the function
check_database
```

Next, add a check for disk space:

```
check_disk_space() {
    echo "Checking disk space..."
    THRESHOLD=80
    USAGE=$(df -h / | grep '/' | awk '{print $5}' | sed
's/%//')
    if [[ $USAGE -gt $THRESHOLD ]]; then
        echo "Warning: Disk usage is at ${USAGE}%."
    else
        echo "Disk usage is at ${USAGE}%, which is within
acceptable limits."
    fi
}
# Call the function
check_disk_space
```

This function warns if disk usage exceeds a defined threshold.

Aggregate Validation Checks

Now, we combine all checks into a comprehensive validation script:

```
#!/bin/bash
echo "Starting dynamic validation..."
# Function definitions...
# Call functions
check_endpoints
check_database
check_disk_space
echo "Dynamic validation completed successfully."
```

If you put the script together using functions, you can build in flexibility so it can keep growing as you need it to.

Integrate Validation into Deployment Workflow

Next, you'll want to add the validation script to the deployment process so that it can automatically check the system's health after deployment.

So to do this, modify **`deploy.sh`** to include validation:

```
#!/bin/bash
echo "Starting deployment process..."
# Deployment steps...
# Perform validation
./health_check.sh
if [[ $? -ne 0 ]]; then
    echo "Validation failed. Initiating rollback..."
    ./rollback.sh "v1.0"
    exit 1
fi
echo "Deployment and validation completed successfully."
```

By running the validation script post-deployment, you ensure that the new deployment hasn't introduced issues.

Schedule Regular Validation

Next, set up a scheduled task to run the validation script at regular intervals. For this, edit the crontab:

```
crontab -e
```

Add the following line to run the validation script every 15 minutes:

```
*/15 * * * * /path/to/health_check.sh >>
/path/to/validation.log 2>&1
```

This configuration schedules the script to run every 15 minutes, logging the output.

Send Alerts on Failure

Finally, configure the script to send notifications if validation fails.

```
send_alert() {
    echo "Validation failed at $(date)" | mail -s "Validation
Alert" team@example.com
}
# Update failure points
if [[ "$response" -ne 200 ]]; then
    echo "Error: $url returned status code $response"
    send_alert
    exit 1
fi
```

Here, you must ensure that the mail utility is configured on your system.

All these scripts give you real-time updates on system health, so you can respond quickly to any issues. Adding validation to your deployment workflows and scheduling regular checks helps you keep your services reliable and your users confident in them.

Summary

In short, we've concentrated on making the testing and validation processes more automated to improve the quality of the software. We've created shell scripts for automated unit and integration tests, which has made the testing workflow much more efficient. This means we can be sure everything is done consistently and any issues are picked up early.

We've created shell scripts for automated testing, making it more efficient and enabling early detection of issues. We've automated code quality checks through linting and static analysis. We've enforced coding standards and caught potential issues early, reducing technical debt. We've also added dynamic validation scripts to our deployment process, so we can be sure that applications and infrastructure are working as expected after deployment.

CHAPTER 4: TASK SCHEDULING AND MONITORING WITH CRONTAB

Overview

In this chapter, we're going to look at how to automate your regular DevOps tasks using scheduling and monitoring. In particular, we will look at how to use CRONTAB to automate tasks like backups, updates, and health checks that you need to do regularly. If you schedule these tasks, they'll all run on time and you will have more bandwidth for other things.

Next, we will learn how to track the success and failure of scheduled jobs using scripts for monitoring tasks. We will create scripts that keep an eye on CRON jobs, create logs, and send alerts when there are any issues. Finally, we're going to look at more advanced scheduling tools and options, beyond CRONTAB. We will explore tools like **`at`**, **`anacron`**, and **`systemd`** timers, which are great for more flexible, less frequent tasks. By the end of this chapter, we will have a good understanding of how to automate and monitor scheduled tasks in a DevOps environment.

Setting up Scheduled Tasks

Among the various tools available, CRONTAB stands out as a widely used utility for scheduling jobs on Unix-like systems. Its simplicity and versatility make it a favorite among DevOps and automation teams. By allowing tasks to run automatically at specified times or intervals, CRONTAB reduces manual intervention and ensures that essential processes like backups, health checks, and log rotations occur consistently.

To begin configuring CRONTAB for automating routine tasks, we will focus on our existing Node.js project. Suppose there are scripts already created for backups (**`backup.sh`**), health checks (**`health_check.sh`**), and log rotations (**`log_rotate.sh`**). These scripts need to be scheduled to run at appropriate times to maintain system health and data integrity.

Understand CRONTAB Syntax

Each CRON job is defined by a line in the CRONTAB file, consisting of five fields representing the time and date, followed by the command to execute:

```
* * * * * command_to_execute
```

The five fields correspond to:

1. **Minute** (0-59)
2. **Hour** (0-23)
3. **Day of Month** (1-31)
4. **Month** (1-12)

5. **Day of Week** (0-6, where 0 is Sunday)

An asterisk (*****) in a field means "every" possible value of that field.

Setting up Backups with CRONTAB

Suppose the **backup.sh** script performs a database backup and saves it to a secure location. So first, ensure the **backup.sh** script is executable:

```
chmod +x backup.sh
```

Next, edit the CRONTAB file:

```
crontab -e
```

Add the following line to schedule the backup script to run every day at 2:00 AM:

```
0 2 * * * /path/to/backup.sh >> /path/to/logs/backup.log 2>&1
```

This line specifies that at minute **0** of hour **2** every day, the **backup.sh** script will execute. The output and errors are appended to **backup.log** for record-keeping.

Automate Health Checks

The **health_check.sh** script, previously created, can be scheduled to run every 15 minutes. Here again, ensure the script is executable:

```
chmod +x health_check.sh
```

Now, edit the CRONTAB file:

```
crontab -e
```

And, add the following line:

```
*/15 * * * * /path/to/health_check.sh >>
/path/to/logs/health_check.log 2>&1
```

The ***/15** in the minute field means the script runs every 15 minutes, ensuring continuous monitoring of application health.

Schedule Log Rotations

It's easy for log files to get out of control, taking up too much space and becoming a hassle to manage. Automating log rotation is a great way to keep your logs manageable. Suppose there's a **log_rotate.sh** script that compresses and archives old logs. You edit the CRONTAB file:

```
crontab -e
```

Add the following line to schedule log rotation every Sunday at midnight:

```
0 0 * * 0 /path/to/log_rotate.sh >>
/path/to/logs/log_rotate.log 2>&1
```

The **0** in the day of the week field represents Sunday. This setup ensures logs are rotated weekly, keeping the system tidy.

Using Environment Variables in CRON Jobs

Sometimes, scripts require specific environment variables. Since CRON jobs have a limited environment, it's necessary to define these variables within the CRONTAB file or within the script.

For example, if **backup.sh** requires database credentials:

```
# In backup.sh
#!/bin/bash
export DB_USER="dbuser"
export DB_PASSWORD="dbpassword"
# Backup command
pg_dump -U $DB_USER -W $DB_PASSWORD mydatabase >
/path/to/backups/db_backup.sql
```

Alternatively, set variables directly in the CRONTAB:

```
0 2 * * * DB_USER=dbuser DB_PASSWORD=dbpassword
/path/to/backup.sh >> /path/to/logs/backup.log 2>&1
```

If you define the variables, the script will run the way you want it to when it's run by CRON.

Schedule Jobs with Special Timing Needs

For tasks that need to run at specific intervals, CRONTAB offers special scheduling options. For instance, to run a script every weekday at 8:30 AM:

```
30 8 * * 1-5 /path/to/weekday_task.sh >>
/path/to/logs/weekday_task.log 2>&1
```

In the above, **1-5** in the day of the week field represents Monday through Friday.

Using System-Wide CRON Directories

For system-wide tasks, place scripts in **/etc/cron.hourly**, **/etc/cron.daily**, **/etc/cron.weekly**, or **/etc/cron.monthly**. The scripts in these directories run automatically at the corresponding intervals.

Here, copy the **health_check.sh** script to the hourly CRON directory:

```
sudo cp health_check.sh /etc/cron.hourly/
```

The **run-parts** utility executes scripts in a directory. It's used by system CRON directories. Here, you need to make sure the scripts in **/etc/cron.*** directories are executable, and do not have extensions like **.sh** (unless **run-parts** is configured to accept them).

Monitoring Scheduled Tasks

While CRONTAB makes it easy to schedule tasks, you still need to keep an eye on these jobs to make sure everything runs smoothly. By getting a monitoring solution up and running, you can spot any problems, collect logs, and get alerts when something goes wrong.

Create a Monitor Script

Let us start by creating a script that checks the status of CRON jobs. And for this let us assume there's a script named **monitor_cron_jobs.sh** that performs this function.

```
#!/bin/bash

echo "Monitoring scheduled tasks..."

# Define the log directory

LOG_DIR="/path/to/logs"

# Define an array of job names and their corresponding log
files

declare -A JOBS

JOBS=(

  ["backup"]="backup.log"
```

```
  ["health_check"]="health_check.log"
  ["log_rotate"]="log_rotate.log"
)
# Loop through each job to check the last execution status
for job in "${!JOBS[@]}"; do
    log_file="$LOG_DIR/${JOBS[$job]}"
    if [[ -f "$log_file" ]]; then
        # Get the last line of the log file
        last_line=$(tail -n 1 "$log_file")
        # Check for success or failure keywords
        if echo "$last_line" | grep -q "completed
successfully"; then
            echo "Job '$job' executed successfully."
        else
            echo "Job '$job' encountered an error."
            # Send an alert (email, SMS, etc.)
            # send_alert "Job '$job' failed. Check the log at
$log_file"
        fi
    else
        echo "Log file for job '$job' not found."
        # send_alert "Log file for job '$job' not found at
$log_file"
    fi
done
chmod +x monitor_cron_jobs.sh
```

This script iterates over defined jobs, checks their log files for success messages, and identifies any failures.

Schedule Monitor Script

Now let us schedule the monitoring script to run at desired intervals, such as every hour.

For this, edit the CRONTAB:

```
crontab -e
```

And, add the following line:

```
0 * * * * /path/to/monitor_cron_jobs.sh >>
/path/to/logs/monitor.log 2>&1
```

This configuration allows to run the monitoring script at the top of every hour.

Implement Alert Notifications

If you want to know when a job fails, you can get alerts by setting up notifications via email or messaging services as below:

Email Alerts

First, configure the **send_alert** function in the monitoring script:

```
send_alert() {
    local message="$1"
    echo "$message" | mail -s "CRON Job Alert"
team@example.com
}
```

SMS or Messaging Apps

For SMS or apps like Slack, you can use their APIs within the **send_alert** function.

Below is a quick example for Slack:

```
send_alert() {
    local message="$1"
    curl -X POST -H 'Content-type: application/json' \
    --data '{"text":"'"$message"'"}' \
    https://hooks.slack.com/services/YOUR/SLACK/WEBHOOK
}
```

Here, replace the webhook URL with your actual Slack incoming webhook URL.

Create a Dashboard for CRON Jobs

For a visual representation, generate a simple dashboard or report. To do this, modify the monitoring script to create an HTML report.

```
# Create an HTML file
report_file="/path/to/reports/cron_report.html"
echo "<html><body><h1>CRON Jobs Status</h1><ul>" >
"$report_file"
for job in "${!JOBS[@]}"; do
    # Check job status...
    if [[ "$status" == "OK" ]]; then
        echo "<li>$job: <span
style='color:green;'>Success</span></li>" >> "$report_file"
    else
        echo "<li>$job: <span
style='color:red;'>Failure</span></li>" >> "$report_file"
    fi
done
echo "</ul></body></html>" >> "$report_file"
```

You can access the report through a web server, if you want.

Implement Retry Mechanisms

When it comes to mission-critical tasks, it's a good idea to set up a system that lets you try again if something goes wrong.

So here, we are going to add retries in CRON Jobs by modifying the CRONTAB entry:

```
0 2 * * * /path/to/retry_wrapper.sh /path/to/backup.sh >>
/path/to/logs/backup.log 2>&1
```

Then we create **retry_wrapper.sh**:

```
#!/bin/bash
```

```
attempt=0
max_attempts=3
while [[ $attempt -lt $max_attempts ]]; do
    "$@"
    if [[ $? -eq 0 ]]; then
        exit 0
    fi
    attempt=$((attempt + 1))
    sleep 60
done
echo "Job failed after $max_attempts attempts."
exit 1
```

This wrapper retries the job up to three times, with a 60-second delay between attempts.

Dynamic Scheduling and CRON Alternatives

While CRONTAB is effective for recurring tasks, certain scenarios require more flexible or less frequent scheduling solutions. Tools like **at** and **anacron** cater to these needs by allowing for one-time or catch-up executions, ensuring critical tasks aren't missed due to system downtime or irregular schedules. If you add these tools to your skill set, you'll be able to automate complex scheduling requirements more easily.

Using 'at' Command

The **at** command schedules a command or script to run once at a specified time in the future. This is ideal for tasks that don't recur regularly but need to execute at a particular moment.

First, ensure the **at** utility is installed:

```
sudo apt install at
```

Nexrt we run **maintenance.sh**, let us say 2:30 AM tomorrow:

```
at 2:30 AM tomorrow -f /path/to/maintenance.sh
```

Alternatively, you can pipe commands into **at**:

```
echo "/path/to/maintenance.sh" | at 2:30 AM tomorrow
```

We can also list the scheduled jobs with:

```
atq
```

We may also remove a scheduled job using its job number:

```
atrm [job_number]
```

Leveraging 'anacron' for Infrequent Tasks

anacron is designed for periodic tasks on systems that don't run continuously, such as laptops or desktops. It ensures scheduled jobs execute at the next available opportunity if the system was off during the scheduled time.

Understanding 'anacron' Syntax

anacron jobs are defined in **/etc/anacrontab** with the format:

```
period delay job-identifier command
```

Here,

- **period**: Frequency in days (**1** for daily, **7** for weekly).
- **delay**: Wait time in minutes after the system starts.
- **job-identifier**: Unique name for the job.
- **command**: Script or command to execute.

Setting up 'anacron' Job

To schedule **weekly_backup.sh** to run weekly, open **/etc/anacrontab** with root privileges, and add the following job:

```
7 10 weekly-backup /path/to/weekly_backup.sh
```

This runs the script every seven days, ten minutes after system startup.

Advanced Schedule with 'systemd' Timers

For systems using **systemd**, timers offer powerful scheduling capabilities, potentially replacing CRONTAB.

Let us first create the service file **/etc/systemd/system/cleanup.service**:

```
[Unit]
Description=Cleanup Service
[Service]
Type=oneshot
ExecStart=/path/to/cleanup.sh
```

Then, now let us create the timer file **/etc/systemd/system/cleanup.timer**:

```
[Unit]
Description=Run cleanup.service daily
[Timer]
OnCalendar=daily
Persistent=true
[Install]
WantedBy=timers.target
```

Now, enable and start the timer:

```
sudo systemctl enable cleanup.timer
sudo systemctl start cleanup.timer
```

Utilize 'batch' Command

The **batch** command schedules commands to run when system load is low.

```
echo "/path/to/heavy_task.sh" | batch
```

This above queues the script to run when the system is less busy, optimizing resource usage.

Event-Driven Schedule with 'inotify'

For tasks triggered by file system events, use **inotifywait** from the **inotify-tools** package.

First, install the inotify tools

```
sudo apt install inotify-tools
```

Next, we'll create an event-driven script.

```
#!/bin/bash
inotifywait -m /path/to/watch -e create |
while read path action file; do
    echo "Detected new file: $file"
    /path/to/process_new_file.sh "$path/$file"
done
```

This monitors a directory and executes a script when new files are added.

Implement Flexible Schedule with 'fcron'

`fcron` combines features of both CRONTAB and **`anacron`**, allowing for more nuanced scheduling.

To implement, first install **`fcron`**

```
sudo apt install fcron
```

Then, use **`fcrontab -e`** to edit the fcron table with syntax like:

```
@ 1d run-parts /etc/cron.daily
```

This will run daily tasks, even if the system was off at the scheduled time.

Summary

To sum up, we've expanded our scheduling capabilities beyond CRONTAB so we can handle more complex and varied automation needs. We've also learned how to use the at command to schedule one-time tasks efficiently, which is great for when you need to automate something on the fly. We've found that using anacron helps us keep important tasks running smoothly on systems that aren't always on, so we can maintain essential operations without any extra work.

We've also looked at more advanced scheduling tools, like systemd timers, which give you really precise control and integrate well with system events. By using event-driven scheduling with tools like inotify, we've been able to automate responses to changes in real time. Putting these tools together gives us a really strong set of scheduling tools, so we can automate tasks flexibly, reliably, and efficiently in lots of different DevOps scenarios.

CHAPTER 5: ORCHESTRATING INFRASTRUCTURE WITH SHELL SCRIPTING

Overview

This chapter is all about how to use shell scripting to get the most out of your infrastructure. We will look at how to automate the setup and teardown of infrastructure, including servers, networks, and services. This automation helps you scale up quickly and keep your environments consistent, which cuts down on the chances of human error during setup tasks that you do over and over.

Next, we will look at how to automate the configuration and maintenance of systems using scripting for configuration management tasks. We will look at how to deploy software, manage configurations, and enforce system states across multiple machines using shell scripts. This approach makes sure that everything's the same and that everyone is following the same policies, which helps to make managing complex infrastructures easier.

Finally, we will look at how to keep track of changes and work together effectively when sharing infrastructure scripts. We will also look at tools like Git that help us manage versions of our scripts, document what they do, and keep track of changes. These are important for working with others, checking what's changed, and keeping our automation reliable over time.

Automating Infrastructure Setup and Tear-Down

The key to making sure everyone's working with the same setup and that resources are managed efficiently is to automate the process of setting up and tearing down infrastructure. Scripting these processes lets you quickly spin up and dismantle infrastructure components, which cuts down on manual effort and minimizes errors. Next, we'll create shell scripts to automate the setup and teardown of the infrastructure for our project. We'll focus on server provisioning, configuration, and resource cleanup.

Provision Servers

To begin automating infrastructure setup, we will create a script that provisions a new server instance. Suppose we're using a cloud provider like AWS, and we have the AWS CLI installed and configured on our local machine.

First, ensure the AWS CLI is installed:

```
aws --version
```

If not installed, follow AWS's documentation to set it up.

Creating Provisioning Script

First, create a script named **provision_server.sh**:

```bash
#!/bin/bash
echo "Starting infrastructure provisioning..."
# Define variables
INSTANCE_TYPE="t2.micro"
AMI_ID="ami-0abcdef1234567890" # Replace with your desired AMI
ID
KEY_NAME="my-key-pair"
SECURITY_GROUP="my-security-group"
# Provision EC2 instance
INSTANCE_ID=$(aws ec2 run-instances \
  --image-id $AMI_ID \
  --count 1 \
  --instance-type $INSTANCE_TYPE \
  --key-name $KEY_NAME \
  --security-groups $SECURITY_GROUP \
  --query 'Instances[0].InstanceId' \
  --output text)
if [[ -z "$INSTANCE_ID" ]]; then
    echo "Failed to provision EC2 instance."
    exit 1
fi
echo "EC2 instance $INSTANCE_ID provisioned successfully."
# Tag the instance
aws ec2 create-tags \
  --resources $INSTANCE_ID \
  --tags Key=Name,Value=myapp-server
echo "Instance tagged with Name=myapp-server."
```

This script automates the creation of an EC2 instance with specified parameters. Replace **AMI_ID**, **KEY_NAME**, and **SECURITY_GROUP** with your actual values.

```
chmod +x provision_server.sh
```

Running Provisioning Script

Next, execute the script:

```
./provision_server.sh
```

The script outputs the progress and confirms the successful provisioning of the server.

Configure Server Automatically

After provisioning the server, it's important to configure it for our application. We will automate the configuration using a shell script that performs tasks like installing dependencies and setting up the application environment.

Creating Configuration Script

Let's create a script named **configure_server.sh**:

```
#!/bin/bash
echo "Starting server configuration..."
# Retrieve the instance's public DNS
INSTANCE_ID=$1
PUBLIC_DNS=$(aws ec2 describe-instances \
  --instance-ids $INSTANCE_ID \
  --query 'Reservations[0].Instances[0].PublicDnsName' \
  --output text)
if [[ -z "$PUBLIC_DNS" ]]; then
    echo "Failed to retrieve public DNS of the instance."
    exit 1
fi
echo "Public DNS: $PUBLIC_DNS"
# Define the setup commands
SETUP_COMMANDS="
sudo apt update &&
```

```
sudo apt install -y git nodejs npm &&
git clone https://github.com/yourusername/yourapp.git &&
cd yourapp &&
npm install &&
pm2 start app.js
"

# Execute the setup commands on the remote server
ssh -o "StrictHostKeyChecking no" -i /path/to/your/key.pem
ubuntu@$PUBLIC_DNS "$SETUP_COMMANDS"
if [[ $? -ne 0 ]]; then
    echo "Server configuration failed."
    exit 1
fi
echo "Server configured successfully."
```

This script connects to the newly provisioned server and performs the necessary setup. Replace **`/path/to/your/key.pem`** with the path to your SSH key and update the Git repository URL accordingly.

```
chmod +x configure_server.sh
```

Running Configuration Script

Next, execute the script with the instance ID obtained from the provisioning script:

```
./configure_server.sh i-0123456789abcdef0
```

This script automates the installation of required software and deployment of the application on the server.

Automate Infrastructure Teardown

To make sure you're managing your resources and costs effectively, it's a good idea to automate the teardown of infrastructure when it's no longer needed.

Creating Teardown Script

Let's create a script named **`teardown_infrastructure.sh`**:

```
#!/bin/bash
echo "Starting infrastructure teardown..."
# Define variables
INSTANCE_ID=$1
if [[ -z "$INSTANCE_ID" ]]; then
    echo "Usage: ./teardown_infrastructure.sh <instance_id>"
    exit 1
fi
# Terminate the EC2 instance
aws ec2 terminate-instances --instance-ids $INSTANCE_ID
if [[ $? -ne 0 ]]; then
    echo "Failed to terminate instance $INSTANCE_ID."
    exit 1
fi
echo "Instance $INSTANCE_ID terminated successfully."
# Optionally, delete other resources like security groups or
key pairs
chmod +x teardown_infrastructure.sh
```

Running Teardown Script

Now, execute the script with the instance ID:

```
./teardown_infrastructure.sh i-0123456789abcdef0
```

This above script terminates the specified EC2 instance, freeing up resources.

Automate Entire Workflow

Combine the provisioning, configuration, and teardown scripts into a single script to manage the entire lifecycle.

Creating Orchestration Script

First, create a script named **manage_infrastructure.sh**:

```bash
#!/bin/bash
echo "Managing infrastructure..."
# Provision server
./provision_server.sh
# Capture the instance ID from the provisioning script output
INSTANCE_ID=$(aws ec2 describe-instances \
  --filters "Name=tag:Name,Values=myapp-server" \
  --query 'Reservations[0].Instances[0].InstanceId' \
  --output text)
if [[ -z "$INSTANCE_ID" ]]; then
    echo "Failed to retrieve instance ID."
    exit 1
fi
# Configure server
./configure_server.sh $INSTANCE_ID
# Optionally, wait for user input before teardown
read -p "Press enter to teardown infrastructure..."
# Teardown infrastructure
./teardown_infrastructure.sh $INSTANCE_ID
chmod +x manage_infrastructure.sh
```

Running Orchestration Script

As usual, execute the script:

```bash
./manage_infrastructure.sh
```

This script automates the entire process from provisioning to teardown, streamlining infrastructure management.

Scripting Configuration Management Tasks

The thing about managing server configurations and environment setups across multiple servers is that it can get pretty complex. That's where shell scripts come in handy. They help us keep things consistent and cut down on manual errors. In this next part, we're going to beef up our scripts to manage configuration files and automate environment setups for our application.

Automate Configuration File Management

Suppose our application requires specific configuration files to be present on the server. We will automate the deployment and management of these files. Here, we will update **configure_server.sh** to include configuration file management:

```
#!/bin/bash

echo "Starting server configuration..."

# Retrieve the instance's public DNS

INSTANCE_ID=$1

PUBLIC_DNS=$(aws ec2 describe-instances \

  --instance-ids $INSTANCE_ID \

  --query 'Reservations[0].Instances[0].PublicDnsName' \

  --output text)

echo "Public DNS: $PUBLIC_DNS"

# Copy configuration files to the server

scp -i /path/to/your/key.pem config/*.json
ubuntu@$PUBLIC_DNS:/home/ubuntu/yourapp/config/

if [[ $? -ne 0 ]]; then

    echo "Failed to copy configuration files."

    exit 1

fi

# Define the setup commands

SETUP_COMMANDS="

sudo mv /home/ubuntu/yourapp/config/*.json
/path/to/app/config/ &&

sudo chown appuser:appgroup /path/to/app/config/*.json

"

# Execute the setup commands on the remote server
```

```
ssh -i /path/to/your/key.pem ubuntu@$PUBLIC_DNS
"$SETUP_COMMANDS"

echo "Configuration files deployed successfully."
```

This copies configuration files from the local **config** directory to the server and moves them to the appropriate location.

Automate Environment Setup

Now, to ensure the server environment is properly configured, automate the installation of environment variables and system settings. We modify **configure_server.sh** to set environment variables:

```
# Set environment variables

ENV_VARS="

export APP_ENV=production

export DB_HOST=yourdbhost

export DB_USER=dbuser

export DB_PASS=dbpassword

"

# Append environment variables to .bashrc

ssh -i /path/to/your/key.pem ubuntu@$PUBLIC_DNS "echo
'$ENV_VARS' >> ~/.bashrc"

echo "Environment variables set successfully."
```

This addition ensures that required environment variables are set for the application to function correctly.

Automate Software Deployment

I'll show you how to use shell scripts to deploy the latest version of your application automatically. All you have to do is create a script named **deploy_app.sh**:

```
#!/bin/bash

echo "Deploying application..."

# Retrieve the instance's public DNS

INSTANCE_ID=$1
```

```
PUBLIC_DNS=$(aws ec2 describe-instances \
  --instance-ids $INSTANCE_ID \
  --query 'Reservations[0].Instances[0].PublicDnsName' \
  --output text)
# Pull the latest code from the repository
ssh -i /path/to/your/key.pem ubuntu@$PUBLIC_DNS "
cd yourapp &&
git pull origin master &&
npm install &&
pm2 restart all
"
echo "Application deployed successfully."
```

This script updates the application code on the server and restarts the application process.

Automate User and Permission Management

You can manage user accounts and permissions via scripts to keep things secure and consistent. To do this, you'll want to add user management to **configure_server.sh**:

```
# Create a new user for the application
ssh -i /path/to/your/key.pem ubuntu@$PUBLIC_DNS "
sudo useradd -m -s /bin/bash appuser &&
sudo chown -R appuser:appuser /home/ubuntu/yourapp
"
echo "User 'appuser' created and permissions set."
```

This ensures that the application runs under a dedicated user account with appropriate permissions.

Automate Firewall Configuration

We can also set up your security group and firewall rules to keep your infrastructure safe by creating a script **configure_firewall.sh**:

```
#!/bin/bash
echo "Configuring firewall..."
# Define variables
SECURITY_GROUP_ID="sg-0abcdef1234567890" # Replace with your security group ID
# Open port 80 for HTTP traffic
aws ec2 authorize-security-group-ingress \
  --group-id $SECURITY_GROUP_ID \
  --protocol tcp \
  --port 80 \
  --cidr 0.0.0.0/0
echo "Firewall configured to allow HTTP traffic."
chmod +x configure_firewall.sh
```

We run the script as below:

```
./configure_firewall.sh
```

Automate Environment Consistency across Multiple Servers

When managing multiple servers, use loops and configuration files to automate tasks across all instances by creating a script named **configure_multiple_servers.sh**:

```
#!/bin/bash
echo "Configuring multiple servers..."
# List of instance IDs
INSTANCE_IDS=("i-0123456789abcdef0" "i-0fedcba9876543210")
for INSTANCE_ID in "${INSTANCE_IDS[@]}"; do
    echo "Configuring instance $INSTANCE_ID..."
    ./configure_server.sh $INSTANCE_ID
done
echo "All servers configured successfully."
```

This script iterates over a list of instance IDs and applies configuration to each one.

Automate with Infrastructure as Code Tools

While shell scripts are powerful, integrating them with tools like Terraform or Ansible enhances automation capabilities. We can integrate shell scripts into Terraform provisioning:

```
resource "aws_instance" "app_server" {
  ami             = "ami-0abcdef1234567890"
  instance_type = "t2.micro"
  key_name        = "my-key-pair"
  security_groups = ["my-security-group"]
  provisioner "remote-exec" {
    inline = [
      "sudo apt update",
      "sudo apt install -y git nodejs npm",
      "git clone https://github.com/yourusername/yourapp.git",
      "cd yourapp",
      "npm install",
      "pm2 start app.js"
    ]
  }
  connection {
    type        = "ssh"
    user        = "ubuntu"
    private_key = file("/path/to/your/key.pem")
    host        = self.public_ip
  }
}
```

This Terraform configuration automates server provisioning and setup, integrating shell commands within the provisioning process.

Version Control and Documentation of Infrastructure Scripts

It's really important to keep track of and document the scripts you use for infrastructure. This helps to make sure that everyone's working in the same way, and that everything's reliable. With version control and good documentation, you can keep an eye on changes, work with other people on the team, and see how your infrastructure's changed over time. Here, we'll look at the best ways to manage the scripts we've been talking about in the last few chapters. We'll focus on using Git for version control and some good documentation techniques.

Using Git

Git and other version control systems let you track changes to your scripts, go back to older versions, and work with others. By putting your infrastructure scripts in a Git repository, you make sure that every change is recorded and can be checked or rolled back if needed.

Initializing a Git Repository

Begin by creating a Git repository for your infrastructure scripts:

```
cd /path/to/your/scripts
git init
```

This command initializes a new Git repository in the current directory.

Adding Scripts to the Repository

Add your scripts to the repository:

```
git add provision_server.sh configure_server.sh
teardown_infrastructure.sh manage_infrastructure.sh
```

Include all relevant scripts and configuration files.

Committing Changes

Commit the added files with a meaningful message:

```
git commit -m "Initial commit of infrastructure scripts"
```

This records the current state of the scripts in the repository.

Using Meaningful Commit Messages

When making changes, write clear and descriptive commit messages that explain the purpose of the changes:

```
git commit -am "Added user management to configure_server.sh"
```

This practice helps others understand the history and reasoning behind modifications.

Branching and Merging

Use branches to develop new features or experiment without affecting the main codebase:

```
git checkout -b feature/add-firewall-config
```

After making changes, merge the branch back into the main branch:

```
git checkout main
git merge feature/add-firewall-config
```

Branches enable multiple team members to work simultaneously without conflicts.

Collaborating with Remote Repositories

Push your repository to a remote service like GitHub or GitLab for collaboration:

```
git remote add origin
https://github.com/yourusername/infrastructure-scripts.git
git push -u origin main
```

This allows team members to clone the repository, contribute, and stay updated.

Document Infrastructure Scripts

Having thorough documentation is really important for understanding how scripts work, how to use them, and how to fix problems. The documentation should be easy to understand and accessible to all team members.

Adding Comments to Scripts

Include comments within your scripts to explain complex sections or important considerations:

```
#!/bin/bash
# This script provisions a new EC2 instance for the
application
```

```
# Define variables
INSTANCE_TYPE="t2.micro"
# AMI_ID corresponds to Ubuntu 20.04 LTS in us-east-1 region
AMI_ID="ami-0abcdef1234567890"
```

Comments help others understand the purpose of variables and commands.

Creating a README File

A **README.md** file provides an overview of the scripts and instructions on how to use them:

````
# Infrastructure Scripts

This repository contains scripts for automating infrastructure provisioning, configuration, and teardown for our Node.js application.

## Scripts

- `provision_server.sh`: Provisions a new EC2 instance.

- `configure_server.sh`: Configures the server with necessary software and application code.

- `teardown_infrastructure.sh`: Terminates the EC2 instance.

- `manage_infrastructure.sh`: Orchestrates provisioning, configuration, and teardown.

## Usage

1. **Provision a Server**

   ```bash

   ./provision_server.sh
````

A README provides essential information for users to get started quickly.

````
**Maintaining a CHANGELOG**

A `CHANGELOG.md` records significant changes, updates, and fixes:

```markdown

# Changelog

## [1.1.0] - 2023-10-01
````

```
### Added
- User management in `configure_server.sh`.
- Firewall configuration script `configure_firewall.sh`.
### Fixed
- Error handling in `provision_server.sh`.
## [1.0.0] - 2023-09-15
- Initial release with basic provisioning and configuration scripts.
```

This helps track the evolution of the scripts over time.

Leverage Git Hooks for Quality Control

I'd suggest using Git hooks to make sure that code quality and standards are up to scratch before committing.

For example, create a **.git/hooks/pre-commit** script:

```
#!/bin/bash
# Run shellcheck on all .sh files
for file in $(git diff --cached --name-only | grep '\.sh$'); do
    shellcheck "$file"
    if [ $? -ne 0 ]; then
        echo "Shellcheck failed on $file"
        exit 1
    fi
done
```

This prevents commits if scripts contain syntax errors or bad practices.

Summary

Overall, we've looked at how to use shell scripting to automate the provisioning, configuration, and teardown of resources, which has made things a lot more efficient. By putting together scripts for setting up and managing the infrastructure, we've learned how to deploy servers, set up environments, and make sure everything is consistent across deployments. The good thing about automating these tasks is that it reduces the manual effort, minimizes errors, and allows for rapid scaling and adaptation in dynamic environments.

On top of all that, we've learned about the best ways to control and record changes to scripts for managing infrastructure. We've made sure that our scripts are easy to maintain and dependable by using Git to track changes and work well with others. With good documentation, it's easier for team members to understand and use the scripts, and to contribute to their development. These practices help us manage complex infrastructures with confidence and precision.

Chapter 6: Incident Resolution and Log Management

Overview

This chapter is all about improving system reliability and responsiveness by using automation. We're going to look into how we can use automation to keep an eye on what's going on with our systems and spot any problems right away. If we automate the detection process, we will know right away when there's something wrong. Then we can jump in and fix it before it gets out of hand.

Next, we will look at Quick Incident Resolution Scripts, where we will learn how to write scripts that can automatically handle some of the most common incidents. By writing scripts to handle common problems like restarting services or cleaning up resources, we reduce downtime and improve system stability. The good thing about automating these responses is that it speeds up recovery time and makes sure everyone's following the same procedures.

Finally, we will look at ways of automating the gathering and analysis of log data. We will learn how to collect logs from different sources, make sense of them, and spot patterns that might show there's a bigger problem. If we automate log management, we can keep an eye on things proactively and make better decisions, which helps our systems stay healthy. All of this helps us detect, respond to, and analyze incidents more quickly and easily.

Automating Incident Detection and Alerts

Why Automation in Incident Detection?

In a fast-changing DevOps setup, it's important to be proactive in spotting problems so we can keep the system reliable and avoid any unplanned downtime. If your application performance is affected by things like high CPU usage, memory leaks, low disk space, or outages, it can really impact the way your business runs. It's not really feasible to monitor everything manually, especially in complex IT environments with lots of servers and services. Automation keeps an eye on things 24/7, cuts down on mistakes, and lets you react faster. Automating incident detection and alerts helps teams spot issues quickly, often before they affect end users. Scripted solutions let you customize the monitoring to fit your needs and integrate it into your existing workflows without any fuss.

Monitor System Metrics

To begin automating incident detection, create scripts that monitor critical system metrics. So we will now develop a script that checks CPU usage, memory usage, and disk space.

```
#!/bin/bash
echo "Starting system monitoring..."
```

```
# Define threshold values
CPU_THRESHOLD=80
MEM_THRESHOLD=80
DISK_THRESHOLD=80
# Check CPU usage
CPU_USAGE=$(top -bn1 | grep "Cpu(s)" | awk '{print 100 - $8}')
CPU_INT=${CPU_USAGE%.*}
if [[ $CPU_INT -gt $CPU_THRESHOLD ]]; then
    echo "High CPU usage detected: $CPU_USAGE%"
    # Trigger alert
    ./send_alert.sh "High CPU usage: $CPU_USAGE%"
fi
# Check Memory usage
MEM_USAGE=$(free | grep Mem | awk '{print $3/$2 * 100.0}')
MEM_INT=${MEM_USAGE%.*}
if [[ $MEM_INT -gt $MEM_THRESHOLD ]]; then
    echo "High Memory usage detected: $MEM_USAGE%"
    # Trigger alert
    ./send_alert.sh "High Memory usage: $MEM_USAGE%"
fi
# Check Disk usage
DISK_USAGE=$(df / | tail -1 | awk '{print $5}' | sed 's/%//')
if [[ $DISK_USAGE -gt $DISK_THRESHOLD ]]; then
    echo "High Disk usage detected: $DISK_USAGE%"
    # Trigger alert
    ./send_alert.sh "High Disk usage: $DISK_USAGE%"
fi
echo "System monitoring completed."
```

This script checks if CPU, memory, or disk usage exceeds defined thresholds and triggers an alert if any do.

```
chmod +x monitor_system.sh
```

Detect Service Status

Next, keeping an eye on the system services is key to making sure that the applications are running smoothly. To do this, we just need to modify **monitor_system.sh** to include service checks.

```
# Define services to monitor
SERVICES=("nginx" "mysql" "redis")
for SERVICE in "${SERVICES[@]}"; do
    if ! systemctl is-active --quiet $SERVICE; then
        echo "Service $SERVICE is not running."
        # Trigger alert
        ./send_alert.sh "Service $SERVICE is down."
    fi
done
```

This loop checks the status of each service and triggers an alert if any are not running.

Automate Alert Triggers

To notify the team when incidents occur, we create an alerting mechanism by creating a script named **send_alert.sh**:

```
#!/bin/bash
MESSAGE=$1
ALERT_METHOD="email" # or "slack", "sms"
send_email() {
    echo "$MESSAGE" | mail -s "Incident Alert"
team@example.com
}
send_slack() {
    curl -X POST -H 'Content-type: application/json' \
```

```
    --data '{"text":"'"$MESSAGE"'"}' \
    https://hooks.slack.com/services/YOUR/SLACK/WEBHOOK
}
case $ALERT_METHOD in
    email)
        send_email
        ;;
    slack)
        send_slack
        ;;
    *)
        echo "No valid alert method specified."
        ;;
esac
```

Here, we replace **YOUR/SLACK/WEBHOOK** with your actual Slack webhook URL and adjust **ALERT_METHOD** as needed.

```
chmod +x send_alert.sh
```

Implement Threshold-Based Alerts

For metrics that fluctuate, we can implement thresholds that consider sustained high usage. To do this, we modify **monitor_system.sh** to check averages over time:

```
# Check CPU usage over the last 5 minutes
CPU_USAGE=$(uptime | awk -F'load average:' '{ print $2 }' |
cut -d, -f1 | xargs)
CPU_INT=${CPU_USAGE%.*}
CPU_THRESHOLD=1.5 # Adjust based on number of CPU cores
if (( $(echo "$CPU_USAGE > $CPU_THRESHOLD" | bc -l) )); then
    echo "High average CPU load detected: $CPU_USAGE"
    ./send_alert.sh "High average CPU load: $CPU_USAGE"
```

```
fi
```

This approach reduces false positives due to brief spikes.

Integrate with Monitor Tools

For more advanced monitoring, we can integrate scripts with tools like Nagios or Zabbix. To make it happen, we will create a Nagios plugin script:

```
#!/bin/bash
# Nagios plugin for CPU usage
CPU_USAGE=$(top -bn1 | grep "Cpu(s)" | awk '{print 100 - $8}')
CPU_INT=${CPU_USAGE%.*}
CPU_THRESHOLD=80
if [[ $CPU_INT -lt $CPU_THRESHOLD ]]; then
    echo "OK - CPU usage is at $CPU_USAGE%"
    exit 0
else
    echo "CRITICAL - CPU usage is at $CPU_USAGE%"
    exit 2
fi
```

Add the above script to Nagios and then configure the checks accordingly.

Quick Incident Resolution Scripts

When things go wrong, it's important to get them fixed quickly to avoid any major problems. If we automate some of the tasks involved in fixing things, it makes the recovery process faster and ensures everyone's on the same page. By writing scripts for things like restarting services, allocating resources, and clearing logs, you can resolve incidents without having to involve people manually.

Automate Service Restarts

Services may crash or become unresponsive due to various issues. We can automate the restart process to restore functionality quickly. For this, we can create a script named **restart_service.sh**:

```
#!/bin/bash
SERVICE_NAME=$1
if [[ -z "$SERVICE_NAME" ]]; then
    echo "Usage: ./restart_service.sh <service_name>"
    exit 1
fi
echo "Attempting to restart $SERVICE_NAME..."
systemctl restart $SERVICE_NAME
if systemctl is-active --quiet $SERVICE_NAME; then
    echo "$SERVICE_NAME restarted successfully."
    # Optionally, send a notification
    ./send_alert.sh "$SERVICE_NAME was restarted
successfully."
else
    echo "Failed to restart $SERVICE_NAME."
    ./send_alert.sh "Failed to restart $SERVICE_NAME."
    exit 1
fi
chmod +x restart_service.sh
```

You can also use the below script to restart the services, if needed:

```
./restart_service.sh nginx
```

Automate Resource Allocation

Applications can fail due to problems such as memory leaks or insufficient resources. Automate resource allocation to mitigate these issues. Let us create a script named **add_swap.sh**:

```
#!/bin/bash
SWAP_SIZE_GB=$1
if [[ -z "$SWAP_SIZE_GB" ]]; then
    echo "Usage: ./add_swap.sh <swap_size_in_gb>"
```

```
    exit 1
fi
echo "Adding $SWAP_SIZE_GB GB of swap space..."
fallocate -l "${SWAP_SIZE_GB}G" /swapfile
chmod 600 /swapfile
mkswap /swapfile
swapon /swapfile
# Add to /etc/fstab
echo '/swapfile none swap sw 0 0' | tee -a /etc/fstab
echo "Swap space added successfully."
chmod +x add_swap.sh
```

Next, run the script to add swap space:

```
sudo ./add_swap.sh 2
```

Automate Log Clearance

If not managed properly, logs can take up significant disk space. To avoid running out of disk space, automate log deletion. We can create a script called **clear_logs.sh**:

```
#!/bin/bash
LOG_DIRS=("/var/log/myapp" "/var/log/nginx")
for DIR in "${LOG_DIRS[@]}"; do
    echo "Clearing logs in $DIR..."
    find "$DIR" -type f -name "*.log" -exec truncate -s 0 {}
\;
done
echo "Log clearance completed."
chmod +x clear_logs.sh
```

Schedule the script to run periodically or trigger it when disk usage is high.

Automate Database Maintenance

If there are any issues with the database, it could cause problems with the application. It'd be a good idea to automate some of the maintenance tasks, like optimising tables or clearing the cache. We can do this in the script **optimize_database.sh**:

```
#!/bin/bash
DB_USER="dbuser"
DB_PASS="dbpassword"
DATABASES=("myapp_db")
for DB in "${DATABASES[@]}"; do
    echo "Optimizing database $DB..."
    mysqlcheck -o -u $DB_USER -p$DB_PASS $DB
done
echo "Database optimization completed."
```

Then, make the script executable:

```
chmod 700 optimize_database.sh
```

Integrate Incident Resolution Scripts with Detection

You can combine the detection and resolution scripts for automated responses. In **monitor_system.sh**, call resolution scripts upon detecting issues:

```
if [[ $DISK_USAGE -gt $DISK_THRESHOLD ]]; then
    echo "High Disk usage detected: $DISK_USAGE%"
    ./clear_logs.sh
    ./send_alert.sh "High Disk usage detected and logs
cleared."
fi
```

Automate User Session Management

If a user is using up too many resources, you can end their session using a script **terminate_sessions.sh**:

```
#!/bin/bash
```

```
THRESHOLD=80

echo "Checking for high resource-consuming sessions..."

ps -eo pid,user,%mem,command --sort=-%mem | awk -v
threshold=$THRESHOLD 'NR>1 { if ($3 > threshold) print $1 }' |
while read PID; do

    echo "Terminating process $PID..."

    kill -9 $PID

    ./send_alert.sh "Terminated process $PID due to high
resource usage."

done

echo "Session termination completed."
```

The great thing about these scripts is that they give your team the power to respond quickly to issues, keep everything running smoothly and make sure your users have a great experience. Bringing these practices into your DevOps workflow helps you to manage your systems better.

Automating Log Collection and Analysis

Effective log management is crucial for diagnosing issues, understanding system behavior, and identifying trends that could indicate underlying problems. Automating the collection, parsing, and analysis of logs allows you to process large volumes of data efficiently and gain insights that inform proactive system management. In this section, we will develop scripts to automate log collection from multiple sources, parse logs to extract meaningful information, and analyze the data to identify patterns and root causes.

Collect Logs from Multiple Sources

If you're working in a distributed environment, your logs might be stored on different servers or services. It's a good idea to automate the process of collecting your logs because that way, you can make sure that all of the relevant data is in one place for analysis. You can create a script called **collect_logs.sh**:

```
#!/bin/bash

echo "Starting log collection..."

# Define servers and log paths

declare -A SERVERS
```

```
SERVERS=(
  ["server1"]="user@server1.example.com"
  ["server2"]="user@server2.example.com"
)
LOG_PATHS=(
  "/var/log/myapp/app.log"
  "/var/log/nginx/access.log"
  "/var/log/nginx/error.log"
)
DEST_DIR="/path/to/centralized/logs"
mkdir -p "$DEST_DIR"
# Collect logs from each server
for SERVER in "${!SERVERS[@]}"; do
  echo "Collecting logs from $SERVER..."
  for LOG_PATH in "${LOG_PATHS[@]}"; do
    scp "${SERVERS[$SERVER]}:$LOG_PATH"
"$DEST_DIR/${SERVER}_$(basename $LOG_PATH)"
    if [[ $? -ne 0 ]]; then
      echo "Failed to collect $LOG_PATH from $SERVER"
    fi
  done
done
echo "Log collection completed."
chmod +x collect_logs.sh
```

This script connects to each server, copies specified log files, and stores them in a centralized directory with filenames indicating their origin.

Parse Logs for Meaningful Data

It can be a bit much dealing with raw logs. Parsing logs to get the relevant info makes analysis easier. The best thing to do is create a script called **parse_logs.sh**:

```
#!/bin/bash
echo "Starting log parsing..."
LOG_DIR="/path/to/centralized/logs"
PARSED_DIR="/path/to/parsed/logs"
mkdir -p "$PARSED_DIR"
# Define patterns to extract
ERROR_PATTERN="ERROR"
WARNING_PATTERN="WARNING"
for LOG_FILE in "$LOG_DIR"/*; do
  BASENAME=$(basename "$LOG_FILE")
  PARSED_FILE="$PARSED_DIR/parsed_$BASENAME"

  echo "Parsing $BASENAME..."

  # Extract errors and warnings
  grep -E "$ERROR_PATTERN|$WARNING_PATTERN" "$LOG_FILE" >
"$PARSED_FILE"

  if [[ $? -eq 0 ]]; then
    echo "Parsed data saved to $PARSED_FILE"
  else
    echo "No matching patterns found in $BASENAME"
  fi
done
echo "Log parsing completed."
chmod +x parse_logs.sh
```

This script scans each collected log file for error and warning patterns, saving the extracted lines to new files for easier analysis.

Automate Log Management Process

To streamline the process, create a master script that orchestrates log collection, parsing, and analysis:

```
#!/bin/bash
echo "Starting log management process..."
# Collect logs
./collect_logs.sh
# Parse logs
./parse_logs.sh
# Analyze logs
./analyze_logs.sh
echo "Log management process completed."
chmod +x log_management.sh
```

Then, schedule the script to run at desired intervals using CRON:

```
0 1 * * * /path/to/log_management.sh >>
/path/to/logs/log_management.log 2>&1
```

This configuration runs the log management process daily at 1 AM.

Summary

In this chapter, we looked at ways to automate key parts of incident management to make sure the system is as reliable as possible. We put together scripts that keep an eye on system metrics and flag up incidents as they happen, so we can spot potential problems quickly. By getting the right alerts out automatically, we made sure the people who needed to know got the info when something unusual happened.

We also put together scripts to help us resolve incidents quickly, like restarting services, reallocating resources, and clearing logs. These scripts helped us avoid any downtime and make sure everyone responded in the same way. Finally, we automated the collection and analysis of logs, which helped us quickly spot trends and root causes. The way we parsed and analyzed the log data was really valuable. It helped us to take proactive measures to prevent future incidents. In short, we were able to keep our systems up and running smoothly with these new automation techniques.

CHAPTER 7: MANAGING NETWORK TRAFFIC AND LOAD BALANCING

Overview

In this chapter, we will take a look at some of the most important parts of managing and balancing network traffic in DevOps environments. First, we will look at how to monitor network traffic using shell scripts. This lets us see how much bandwidth is being used, spot any bottlenecks, and identify unusual patterns that could be a sign of security issues or performance problems. Next, we will look at how to automate load balancer configuration. If we script the setup and modification of load balancers, we can efficiently distribute network traffic across multiple servers, ensuring high availability and optimal resource utilization. If we automate this process, we can cut down on manual errors and adjust things on the fly to match changing traffic demands.

Finally, we will look at how to create failover and traffic redirection scripts. Scripts like this let us automatically reroute traffic if a server fails or the network goes down, which is great for keeping service going. The good thing about having automated failover mechanisms in place is that it makes our applications more resilient and means that end users can still access them seamlessly even if there are unexpected disruptions. By the end of this chapter, you will know how to manage network traffic effectively and use shell scripting to implement strong load balancing solutions. This will improve the performance and reliability of your systems.

Traffic Monitoring with Shell Scripts

When it comes to network admin and DevOps, a lot of people use shell scripting to monitor network traffic. It's a popular choice for a few reasons. It's flexible and lets professionals tweak monitoring solutions to fit their specific needs. No need to get bogged down in complex software. You can use shell scripts to set up your own monitoring tools that fit in with the systems you already have. The fact that shell scripting is simple and can be used everywhere makes it a good, efficient option for managing network traffic effectively.

Implement Network Traffic Monitoring

To monitor network traffic using shell scripts, tools like **`netstat`**, **`iftop`**, **`nload`**, and **`tcpdump`** can be leveraged. These utilities provide real-time data on network interfaces, bandwidth usage, and detailed packet information. By scripting around these tools, automated data collection and analysis become feasible.

Before you get started, be sure to install following necessary tools:

- net-tools package (for netstat)
- iftop
- nload
- tcpdump

Monitoring Bandwidth Usage

Monitoring bandwidth usage helps in understanding the network load and identifying potential bottlenecks. The **iftop** utility provides a real-time display of network bandwidth.

First, create a script named **monitor_bandwidth.sh**:

```
#!/bin/bash
# Starting bandwidth monitoring
echo "Starting bandwidth monitoring..."
# Define the network interface to monitor
INTERFACE="eth0"
# Check if iftop is installed
if ! command -v iftop &> /dev/null; then
    echo "iftop is not installed. Installing now..."
    sudo apt-get install iftop -y
fi
# Run iftop in batch mode for a specified duration
DURATION=60  # Duration in seconds
sudo iftop -i $INTERFACE -t -s $DURATION -o 2s -L 10 >
bandwidth_usage.txt
echo "Bandwidth monitoring completed. Data saved to
bandwidth_usage.txt"
```

This script monitors the **eth0** interface for 60 seconds and saves the bandwidth usage details to **bandwidth_usage.txt**.

Monitoring Active Connections

Understanding active network connections aids in identifying unauthorized access or unusual activity. The **netstat** command provides detailed information on network connections.

```
#!/bin/bash
# Collecting active network connections
echo "Collecting active network connections..."
# Capture the current active connections
```

```
netstat -tunap > network_connections.txt
echo "Active network connections saved to
network_connections.txt"
```

Capturing Packet Data

For in-depth analysis, capturing packet data is essential. The **tcpdump** utility allows for capturing and inspecting network packets. For this, create a script named **capture_packets.sh**:

```
#!/bin/bash
# Starting packet capture
echo "Starting packet capture..."
# Define variables
INTERFACE="eth0"
CAPTURE_DURATION=60  # Duration in seconds
OUTPUT_FILE="packet_capture.pcap"
# Check if tcpdump is installed
if ! command -v tcpdump &> /dev/null; then
    echo "tcpdump is not installed. Installing now..."
    sudo apt-get install tcpdump -y
fi
# Start packet capture
sudo timeout $CAPTURE_DURATION tcpdump -i $INTERFACE -w
$OUTPUT_FILE
echo "Packet capture completed. Data saved to $OUTPUT_FILE"
```

Visualize and Log Inbound and Outbound Traffic

Visualizing network traffic helps in identifying patterns and anomalies. Tools like **gnuplot** can be used to create graphical representations of the collected data.

Processing Bandwidth Data

To do this, first extract relevant data from **bandwidth_usage.txt** for visualization.

```
grep -E '=>|<=|Total send rate|Total receive rate'
bandwidth_usage.txt > parsed_bandwidth.txt
```

This command filters lines containing bandwidth information.

Visualizing Bandwidth Usage

Then, use **gnuplot** to create graphs from the parsed data.

```
sudo apt-get install gnuplot -y
```

Format the data appropriately:

```
awk '/Total send rate/ {print $5}' parsed_bandwidth.txt >
send_rate.dat

awk '/Total receive rate/ {print $5}' parsed_bandwidth.txt >
receive_rate.dat
```

Then, create a file named **plot_bandwidth.gp**:

```
set terminal png size 800,600
set output 'bandwidth_usage.png'
set title 'Bandwidth Usage Over Time'
set xlabel 'Time (seconds)'
set ylabel 'Rate (KB/s)'
set grid
plot 'send_rate.dat' title 'Outbound Traffic' with lines, \
     'receive_rate.dat' title 'Inbound Traffic' with lines
```

Then generate the graph:

```
gnuplot plot_bandwidth.gp
```

The graph **bandwidth_usage.png** illustrates inbound and outbound traffic over the monitoring period.

Automate Continuous Monitoring

To maintain ongoing monitoring, schedule the scripts using CRON. First, edit the crontab file:

```
crontab -e
```

Then, add the following entries:

```
# Monitor bandwidth every hour
0 * * * * /path/to/monitor_bandwidth.sh
# Monitor active connections every 15 minutes
*/15 * * * * /path/to/monitor_connections.sh
# Capture packets daily at midnight
0 0 * * * /path/to/capture_packets.sh
```

To prevent logs from consuming excessive disk space, configure log rotation by creating a file **/etc/logrotate.d/network_logs**:

```
/path/to/*.txt /path/to/*.dat {
    daily
    rotate 7
    compress
    missingok
    notifempty
}
```

For more advanced monitoring, consider integrating tools like **vnStat** or **nethogs**.

```
sudo apt-get install vnstat -y
sudo vnstat -u -i eth0
```

Then, create a vnStat monitoring script:

```
#!/bin/bash
# Starting vnStat monitoring
echo "Updating vnStat database..."
sudo vnstat -u -i eth0
# Generate a report
```

```
vnstat -i eth0 -h > vnstat_hourly.txt
echo "vnStat report saved to vnstat_hourly.txt"
```

These scripts help us collect and visualize inbound and outbound traffic data, which makes it easier to manage the network proactively. If we automate these monitoring tasks, we can stay on top of the network conditions all the time, which helps us find and fix any issues quickly.

Automating Load Balancer Configuration

Understand the Need for Automation

Load balancers distribute incoming traffic across multiple servers, preventing any single server from becoming a bottleneck. Manual configuration of load balancers can be time-consuming and error-prone, especially in environments where server instances are frequently added or removed. Automating the configuration and update of load balancers allows for dynamic scaling and adaptability to changes in traffic load. Automation ensures that the load balancer's configuration stays up-to-date with the current state of the backend servers, enabling seamless scaling and consistent performance.

Setting up HAProxy

Before automating the configuration, set up HAProxy on a dedicated server or an existing server acting as the load balancer.

```
sudo apt-get update
sudo apt-get install haproxy -y
haproxy -v
```

The output should display the installed HAProxy version.

Configure HAProxy Manually

Create an initial HAProxy configuration file to establish a baseline.

Following is the sample configuration:

```
sudo nano /etc/haproxy/haproxy.cfg
global
    log /dev/log    local0
    maxconn 4096
```

```
    user haproxy
    group haproxy
    daemon
defaults
    log     global
    mode    http
    option  httplog
    option  dontlognull
    timeout connect 5000
    timeout client  50000
    timeout server  50000
frontend http_front
    bind *:80
    default_backend http_back
backend http_back
    balance roundrobin
    server app1 192.168.1.101:80 check
    server app2 192.168.1.102:80 check
```

This configuration sets up a basic load balancer distributing traffic between two backend servers (**app1** and **app2**).

Now let us start the HAProxy:

```
sudo systemctl enable haproxy
sudo systemctl start haproxy
```

Automate Backend Server Updates

To keep up with changes in traffic load, you can automate the process of adding or removing backend servers from the HAProxy configuration.

First, create a script named **update_haproxy.sh**:

```
#!/bin/bash
echo "Updating HAProxy configuration..."
# Define the path to the HAProxy configuration file
HAPROXY_CFG="/etc/haproxy/haproxy.cfg"
# Define the backend server list file
SERVER_LIST="backend_servers.txt"
# Check if the server list file exists
if [[ ! -f "$SERVER_LIST" ]]; then
    echo "Server list file $SERVER_LIST not found."
    exit 1
fi
# Create a temporary configuration file
TEMP_CFG="/tmp/haproxy.cfg.tmp"
# Copy the static parts of the configuration
grep -B 10000 "backend http_back" "$HAPROXY_CFG" > "$TEMP_CFG"
# Add the backend definition
echo "backend http_back" >> "$TEMP_CFG"
echo "    balance roundrobin" >> "$TEMP_CFG"
# Read the server list and add to the configuration
SERVER_ID=1
while read -r SERVER_IP; do
    if [[ -n "$SERVER_IP" ]]; then
        echo "    server app$SERVER_ID $SERVER_IP:80 check" >>
"$TEMP_CFG"
        ((SERVER_ID++))
    fi
done < "$SERVER_LIST"
# Replace the old configuration with the new one
sudo mv "$TEMP_CFG" "$HAPROXY_CFG"
```

```
# Validate the new configuration
sudo haproxy -c -f "$HAPROXY_CFG"
if [[ $? -ne 0 ]]; then
    echo "New HAProxy configuration is invalid."
    exit 1
fi
# Reload HAProxy to apply changes
sudo systemctl reload haproxy
echo "HAProxy configuration updated successfully."
```

Now, create a file named **backend_servers.txt** containing the IP addresses of backend servers:

```
192.168.1.101
192.168.1.102
./update_haproxy.sh
```

This above script automates the process of updating the HAProxy configuration based on the list of backend servers in **backend_servers.txt**.

Automate Scale Based on Traffic Load

To keep up with changing traffic loads, it's a good idea to integrate the load balancer configuration script with the server provisioning scripts.

As we mentioned earlier, we have **provision_server.sh** and **teardown_infrastructure.sh** scripts for adding and removing servers.

So, update **provision_server.sh** to append the new server's IP to **backend_servers.txt** and update HAProxy:

```
# At the end of the provisioning script
# Get the new server's IP address
NEW_SERVER_IP=$(aws ec2 describe-instances \
  --instance-ids $INSTANCE_ID \
  --query 'Reservations[0].Instances[0].PrivateIpAddress' \
```

```
  --output text)
# Add the new server IP to the backend server list
echo "$NEW_SERVER_IP" >> backend_servers.txt
# Update HAProxy configuration
./update_haproxy.sh
```

And then, update **teardown_infrastructure.sh** to remove the server's IP from **backend_servers.txt** and update HAProxy:

```
# At the end of the teardown script
# Get the server's IP address before termination
SERVER_IP=$(aws ec2 describe-instances \
  --instance-ids $INSTANCE_ID \
  --query 'Reservations[0].Instances[0].PrivateIpAddress' \
  --output text)
# Remove the server IP from the backend server list
sed -i "/$SERVER_IP/d" backend_servers.txt
# Update HAProxy configuration
./update_haproxy.sh
```

Implement Auto Scale Policies

To automate scaling based on traffic, keep an eye on things like CPU usage and set up provisioning or teardown as needed.

So now, create a scaling script named **auto_scale.sh**:

```
#!/bin/bash
echo "Checking system load for auto scaling..."
# Define thresholds
SCALE_UP_THRESHOLD=70
SCALE_DOWN_THRESHOLD=30
MAX_SERVERS=5
MIN_SERVERS=2
```

```
# Get average CPU usage across backend servers
TOTAL_CPU=0
SERVER_COUNT=0
while read -r SERVER_IP; do
    if [[ -n "$SERVER_IP" ]]; then
        CPU_USAGE=$(ssh -o "StrictHostKeyChecking no"
ubuntu@$SERVER_IP "mpstat 1 1 | awk '/Average/ {print 100 -
\$NF}'")
        TOTAL_CPU=$(echo "$TOTAL_CPU + $CPU_USAGE" | bc)
        ((SERVER_COUNT++))
    fi
done < backend_servers.txt
if [[ $SERVER_COUNT -eq 0 ]]; then
    echo "No backend servers available."
    exit 1
fi
AVERAGE_CPU=$(echo "$TOTAL_CPU / $SERVER_COUNT" | bc)
echo "Average CPU usage across $SERVER_COUNT servers:
$AVERAGE_CPU%"
if [[ $AVERAGE_CPU -gt $SCALE_UP_THRESHOLD ]] && [[
$SERVER_COUNT -lt $MAX_SERVERS ]]; then
    echo "Scaling up: Provisioning a new server..."
    ./provision_server.sh
elif [[ $AVERAGE_CPU -lt $SCALE_DOWN_THRESHOLD ]] && [[
$SERVER_COUNT -gt $MIN_SERVERS ]]; then
    echo "Scaling down: Terminating a server..."
    # Select the last server in the list to terminate
    LAST_SERVER_IP=$(tail -n 1 backend_servers.txt)
    INSTANCE_ID=$(aws ec2 describe-instances \
      --filters "Name=private-ip-
address,Values=$LAST_SERVER_IP" \
```

```
        --query 'Reservations[0].Instances[0].InstanceId' \
        --output text)
    ./teardown_infrastructure.sh $INSTANCE_ID
else
    echo "No scaling action required."
fi
```

Next, schedule the **auto_scale.sh** script to run every 5 minutes:

```
*/5 * * * * /path/to/auto_scale.sh >>
/path/to/logs/auto_scale.log 2>&1
```

Automate Load Balancer Configuration in Cloud

If using cloud-based load balancers like AWS Elastic Load Balancer (ELB), use the cloud provider's CLI tools to automate configuration.

Here, create a script named **update_elb.sh** to register instances with ELB:

```
#!/bin/bash
echo "Updating AWS ELB configuration..."
# Define variables
ELB_NAME="myapp-elb"
# Get the list of instance IDs from backend_servers.txt
INSTANCE_IDS=()
while read -r SERVER_IP; do
    if [[ -n "$SERVER_IP" ]]; then
        INSTANCE_ID=$(aws ec2 describe-instances \
            --filters "Name=private-ip-
address,Values=$SERVER_IP" \
            --query 'Reservations[0].Instances[0].InstanceId' \
            --output text)
        INSTANCE_IDS+=("$INSTANCE_ID")
    fi
```

```
done < backend_servers.txt
# Register instances with ELB
aws elb register-instances-with-load-balancer \
    --load-balancer-name $ELB_NAME \
    --instances "${INSTANCE_IDS[@]}"
echo "AWS ELB configuration updated successfully."
```

Then, update the scripts to call **`update_elb.sh`** after adding or removing instances.

```
./update_elb.sh
```

Integrate with Configuration Management Tools

If you're working in a complex environment, you might want to think about integrating scripts with tools like Ansible or Terraform.

In this example, we're going to create an Ansible playbook that manages HAProxy configuration and uses templates to generate the configuration file based on variables.

```
- hosts: haproxy_server
  become: yes
  tasks:
    - name: Generate HAProxy configuration
      template:
        src: haproxy.cfg.j2
        dest: /etc/haproxy/haproxy.cfg
      notify:
        - Restart HAProxy
  handlers:
    - name: Restart HAProxy
      service:
        name: haproxy
        state: restarted
```

Following is the template file (`haproxy.cfg.j2`):

```
global
    log /dev/log    local0
    maxconn 4096
    user haproxy
    group haproxy
    daemon
defaults
    log     global
    mode    http
    option  httplog
    option  dontlognull
    timeout connect 5000
    timeout client  50000
    timeout server  50000
frontend http_front
    bind *:80
    default_backend http_back
backend http_back
    balance roundrobin
    {% for server in backend_servers %}
    server {{ server.name }} {{ server.ip }}:80 check
    {% endfor %}
```

Then, run the playbook:

```
ansible-playbook -i inventory.ini update_haproxy.yml -e
'{"backend_servers": [{"name": "app1", "ip": "192.168.1.101"},
{"name": "app2", "ip": "192.168.1.102"}]}'
```

By using shell scripts to automate your load balancer configuration, you can take advantage of dynamic scaling and handle traffic changes more efficiently. If you link these scripts to your provisioning and scaling tools, they'll make sure that your app infrastructure can cope easily with different loads.

Failover and Traffic Redirection Scripts

In any system that needs to be up and running all the time, it's really important to make sure that it doesn't go down. If a server fails or the network goes down, you need to be able to switch over to another server automatically so that users can still access the system. You can do this by writing shell scripts to redirect traffic and switch over to another server automatically. This makes your system more reliable. In this topic, we'll look at how to set up failover strategies using shell scripting, with examples using tools like HAProxy and DNS updates.

Implement Failover with HAProxy

HAProxy can be configured to detect backend server failures and redirect traffic accordingly. We will enhance our previous HAProxy setup to include health checks and failover configurations.

Configuring Health Checks

We first update the **`haproxy.cfg`** file to include advanced health checks:

```
backend http_back
    balance roundrobin
    option httpchk GET /health
    server app1 192.168.1.101:80 check inter 2000 rise 2 fall
3
    server app2 192.168.1.102:80 check inter 2000 rise 2 fall
3
```

Here,

- **`option httpchk GET /health`**: Sends HTTP GET requests to **`/health`** endpoint to check server health.
- **`check inter 2000`**: Sets the interval between health checks to 2000 milliseconds.
- **`rise 2`**: The server is marked up after two consecutive successful health checks.
- **`fall 3`**: The server is marked down after three consecutive failed health checks.

While you do, ensure that your application exposes a **`/health`** endpoint that returns a 200 OK status when the server is healthy.

Automating HAProxy Reloads

Here, let us first create a script named **reload_haproxy.sh**:

```
#!/bin/bash
echo "Reloading HAProxy configuration..."
sudo haproxy -c -f /etc/haproxy/haproxy.cfg
if [[ $? -ne 0 ]]; then
    echo "Configuration validation failed."
    exit 1
fi
sudo systemctl reload haproxy
echo "HAProxy reloaded successfully."
```

Monitoring Server Health and Triggering Failover

Although HAProxy performs health checks, you can create scripts to monitor servers and adjust configurations dynamically.

So here lt us first create a failover script named **monitor_servers.sh**:

```
#!/bin/bash
echo "Monitoring backend servers..."
SERVER_LIST=("192.168.1.101" "192.168.1.102")
DOWN_SERVERS=()
for SERVER_IP in "${SERVER_LIST[@]}"; do
    HTTP_STATUS=$(curl -s -o /dev/null -w "%{http_code}"
http://$SERVER_IP/health)
    if [[ "$HTTP_STATUS" -ne 200 ]]; then
        echo "Server $SERVER_IP is down."
        DOWN_SERVERS+=("$SERVER_IP")
    else
        echo "Server $SERVER_IP is up."
    fi
```

```
done
if [[ ${#DOWN_SERVERS[@]} -gt 0 ]]; then
    echo "Updating HAProxy configuration to remove down
servers..."
    # Update backend_servers.txt
    for DOWN_SERVER in "${DOWN_SERVERS[@]}"; do
        sed -i "/$DOWN_SERVER/d" backend_servers.txt
    done
    # Update HAProxy configuration
    ./update_haproxy.sh
fi
```

Next, schedule the script to run every minute:

```
* * * * * /path/to/monitor_servers.sh >>
/path/to/logs/monitor_servers.log 2>&1
```

Implement DNS-Based Failover

If you've got more than one load balancer or need to redirect traffic at the DNS level, automating DNS updates can help you switch over in case of a failure.

Now, create a DNS failover script named **dns_failover.sh**:

```
#!/bin/bash
echo "Initiating DNS failover..."
# Define variables
HOSTED_ZONE_ID="ZABCDEFGHIJKLMN"
RECORD_NAME="www.example.com."
PRIMARY_IP="203.0.113.1"
SECONDARY_IP="203.0.113.2"
# Check if the primary server is up
HTTP_STATUS=$(curl -s -o /dev/null -w "%{http_code}"
http://$PRIMARY_IP/health)
```

```
if [[ "$HTTP_STATUS" -ne 200 ]]; then
    echo "Primary server is down. Switching DNS to secondary
server."
    # Create a JSON file for the DNS update
    cat > dns_change.json << EOF
{
    "Comment": "Failover to secondary server",
    "Changes": [
        {
            "Action": "UPSERT",
            "ResourceRecordSet": {
                "Name": "$RECORD_NAME",
                "Type": "A",
                "TTL": 60,
                "ResourceRecords": [
                    {
                        "Value": "$SECONDARY_IP"
                    }
                ]
            }
        }
    ]
}
EOF
    # Update the DNS record
    aws route53 change-resource-record-sets \
        --hosted-zone-id $HOSTED_ZONE_ID \
        --change-batch file://dns_change.json
    echo "DNS failover completed."
```

```
else
    echo "Primary server is up. No action required."
fi
```

Then, schedule the script to run every minute:

```
* * * * * /path/to/dns_failover.sh >>
/path/to/logs/dns_failover.log 2>&1
```

IP Routing Failover with 'Keepalived'

For high availability at the network layer, use VRRP (Virtual Router Redundancy Protocol) with tools like Keepalived.

To begin with, first install Keepalived:

```
sudo apt-get install keepalived -y
```

Then, edit **/etc/keepalived/keepalived.conf** on both servers.

```
vrrp_instance VI_1 {
    state MASTER
    interface eth0
    virtual_router_id 51
    priority 100
    advert_int 1
    authentication {
        auth_type PASS
        auth_pass password
    }
    virtual_ipaddress {
        192.168.1.100
    }
}
```

Change **state** to **BACKUP** and **priority** to **90** on secondary server. And then restart the keepalived.

```
sudo systemctl enable keepalived
sudo systemctl start keepalived
```

The virtual IP **192.168.1.100** will float between the two servers based on their state.

Automate Failover Actions

Next, we manage application state during failover. And for this, we create a failover action script:

```
#!/bin/bash
ACTION=$1
if [[ "$ACTION" == "MASTER" ]]; then
    echo "Transitioning to MASTER state."
    # Start application services
    sudo systemctl start myapp.service
elif [[ "$ACTION" == "BACKUP" ]]; then
    echo "Transitioning to BACKUP state."
    # Stop application services
    sudo systemctl stop myapp.service
fi
```

Then, edit **/etc/keepalived/keepalived.conf** to include **notify** scripts:

```
notify_master "/path/to/failover_action.sh MASTER"
notify_backup "/path/to/failover_action.sh BACKUP"
```

And then finally add email notifications by adding in the **failover scripts**:

```
echo "Failover event occurred" | mail -s "Failover Alert"
admin@example.com
```

By automating failover and traffic redirection, you enhance the robustness of your infrastructure. These scripts ensure that your services remain available despite server failures or network issues, providing a reliable experience to users.

Summary

To wrap things up, we looked at ways to manage network traffic and load balance using shell scripting. We started off by looking at how to keep an eye on network traffic, using scripts to collect and show inbound and outbound data. This helped us understand how we were using bandwidth and spot any problems or unusual patterns. We also looked at ways of keeping on top of the management of your network. This can help to keep everything running as smoothly as possible.

Next, we looked at automating load balancer configuration, using HAProxy in particular. We created scripts to easily add or remove back-end servers so our systems could adapt to changing traffic loads. Finally, we set up failover and traffic redirection scripts to keep everything running smoothly. We made these scripts detect server failures and redirect traffic automatically, so we could avoid any downtime. By doing all this, we made our systems more reliable and efficient, and we can now deliver a great service consistently.

CHAPTER 8: CONTAINERIZATION AND SHELL SCRIPTING

Overview

This chapter is all about containerization and how shell scripting is a key part of managing containerized environments. We will start by looking at how to script container deployment using tools like Docker and Podman. I will show you how to automate the creation and management of containers, which makes it easier to deploy and ensures consistency across different environments.

Next, we will look at how to manage containers and orchestration using shell scripts. We will also look at how to automate tasks like starting, stopping, and monitoring containers, as well as handling networking and storage configurations. This automation makes things more efficient and reduces the chance of human error in container operations.

Finally, we will look at automating Kubernetes deployment and management. We will be looking at Kubernetes and by scripting its deployment and management, we can handle complex cluster operations with ease. We will learn how to automate the setup of Kubernetes clusters, deploy applications, and manage resources effectively using shell scripts. With these skills, we will be able to efficiently manage containerized applications and orchestrate complex deployments.

Container Deployment with Docker and Podman

The container revolution is here. It's changing how we develop, package, and deploy apps. Docker and Podman are two awesome tools that let developers and DevOps engineers create and manage containers like pros. So, we're going to set up Docker and Podman on our system. Then, we'll use them to automate container deployment, configuration, and environment variable management.

Install Docker

Docker is a widely-used platform for containerization, allowing you to package applications with all their dependencies into a standardized unit for software development.

- Update Package Index

Before installing Docker, update your existing list of packages:

```
sudo apt-get update
```

- Install Necessary Packages

Install packages that allow **apt** to use repositories over HTTPS:

```
sudo apt-get install \
```

```
    apt-transport-https \
    ca-certificates \
    curl \
    gnupg \
    lsb-release
```

- Add Docker's Official GPG Key

```
curl -fsSL https://download.docker.com/linux/ubuntu/gpg | sudo
gpg --dearmor -o /usr/share/keyrings/docker-archive-
keyring.gpg
```

- Setup the Stable Repository

```
echo \
  "deb [arch=$(dpkg --print-architecture) signed-
by=/usr/share/keyrings/docker-archive-keyring.gpg] \
  https://download.docker.com/linux/ubuntu \
  $(lsb_release -cs) stable" | sudo tee
/etc/apt/sources.list.d/docker.list > /dev/null
```

- Install Docker Engine

Update the package index again and install Docker Engine:

```
sudo apt-get update
sudo apt-get install docker-ce docker-ce-cli containerd.io
```

- Verify Docker Installation

Check if Docker is installed correctly by running:

```
sudo docker run hello-world
```

This command downloads and runs a test image in a container, confirming that Docker is working.

Install Podman

Podman is an open-source, daemon-less, and rootless container engine that offers a Docker-compatible command-line interface.

- Update the Package Index

```
sudo apt-get update
```

- Install Podman

```
sudo apt-get -y install podman
```

- Verify Podman Installation

Run the following command to check the installation:

```
podman run hello-world
```

If the output displays a welcome message from the **hello-world** container, Podman is installed correctly.

Automate Container Deployment with Docker

Now that Docker is installed, we will now automate container deployment using shell scripts.

- Create a Dockerfile

A **Dockerfile** contains instructions to build a Docker image.

Create a file named **Dockerfile**:

```
# Use an official Node.js runtime as a parent image
FROM node:14
# Set the working directory
WORKDIR /usr/src/app
# Copy package.json and package-lock.json
COPY package*.json ./
# Install dependencies
RUN npm install
# Copy the rest of the application code
COPY . .
# Expose the application port
```

```
EXPOSE 8080
# Define environment variable
ENV NODE_ENV=production
# Start the application
CMD [ "node", "app.js" ]
```

- Build the Docker Image

Create a script named **build_image.sh**:

```
#!/bin/bash
IMAGE_NAME="myapp"
IMAGE_TAG="v1.0"
echo "Building Docker image..."
docker build -t $IMAGE_NAME:$IMAGE_TAG .
if [ $? -eq 0 ]; then
    echo "Docker image built successfully:
$IMAGE_NAME:$IMAGE_TAG"
else
    echo "Failed to build Docker image."
    exit 1
fi
chmod +x build_image.sh
```

- Run the Docker Container with Environment Variables

For this, create a script named **run_container.sh**:

```
#!/bin/bash
IMAGE_NAME="myapp"
IMAGE_TAG="v1.0"
CONTAINER_NAME="myapp_container"
# Define environment variables
```

```
ENV_VARS="-e DB_HOST=db.example.com -e DB_USER=dbuser -e
DB_PASS=dbpassword"
echo "Running Docker container..."
docker run -d --name $CONTAINER_NAME -p 8080:8080 $ENV_VARS
$IMAGE_NAME:$IMAGE_TAG
if [ $? -eq 0 ]; then
    echo "Docker container started successfully:
$CONTAINER_NAME"
else
    echo "Failed to start Docker container."
    exit 1
fi
chmod +x run_container.sh
```

This script runs the Docker container with specified environment variables.

- Automate Container Management

Now create a script named **manage_container.sh**:

```
#!/bin/bash
CONTAINER_NAME="myapp_container"
case "$1" in
    start)
        echo "Starting container..."
        docker start $CONTAINER_NAME
        ;;
    stop)
        echo "Stopping container..."
        docker stop $CONTAINER_NAME
        ;;
    restart)
        echo "Restarting container..."
```

```
        docker restart $CONTAINER_NAME
        ;;
    status)
        docker ps -a | grep $CONTAINER_NAME
        ;;
    logs)
        docker logs -f $CONTAINER_NAME
        ;;
    *)
        echo "Usage: $0 {start|stop|restart|status|logs}"
        exit 1
        ;;
esac
chmod +x manage_container.sh
```

Use the following script to manage the container:

```
./manage_container.sh start
./manage_container.sh status
./manage_container.sh logs
```

Automate Container Deployment with Podman

Create a Containerfile

Podman uses **Containerfile**, which is similar to a **Dockerfile**. For this, create a file named **Containerfile** (you can use the same content as the Dockerfile):

```
# Use an official Node.js runtime as a parent image
FROM node:14
# Set the working directory
WORKDIR /usr/src/app
# Copy package.json and package-lock.json
```

```
COPY package*.json ./
# Install dependencies
RUN npm install
# Copy the rest of the application code
COPY . .
# Expose the application port
EXPOSE 8080
# Define environment variable
ENV NODE_ENV=production
# Start the application
CMD [ "node", "app.js" ]
```

Build the Podman Image

Create a script named **build_podman_image.sh**:

```
#!/bin/bash
IMAGE_NAME="myapp_podman"
IMAGE_TAG="v1.0"
echo "Building Podman image..."
podman build -t $IMAGE_NAME:$IMAGE_TAG -f Containerfile .
if [ $? -eq 0 ]; then
    echo "Podman image built successfully:
$IMAGE_NAME:$IMAGE_TAG"
else
    echo "Failed to build Podman image."
    exit 1
fi
chmod +x build_podman_image.sh
```

Run Podman Container with Environment Variables

Create a script named **run_podman_container.sh**:

```
#!/bin/bash
IMAGE_NAME="myapp_podman"
IMAGE_TAG="v1.0"
CONTAINER_NAME="myapp_podman_container"
# Define environment variables
ENV_VARS="-e DB_HOST=db.example.com -e DB_USER=dbuser -e
DB_PASS=dbpassword"
echo "Running Podman container..."
podman run -d --name $CONTAINER_NAME -p 8080:8080 $ENV_VARS
$IMAGE_NAME:$IMAGE_TAG
if [ $? -eq 0 ]; then
    echo "Podman container started successfully:
$CONTAINER_NAME"
else
    echo "Failed to start Podman container."
    exit 1
fi
chmod +x run_podman_container.sh
./run_podman_container.sh
```

Automate Podman Container Management

Create a script named **manage_podman_container.sh**:

```
#!/bin/bash
CONTAINER_NAME="myapp_podman_container"
case "$1" in
    start)
        echo "Starting container..."
        podman start $CONTAINER_NAME
        ;;
    stop)
```

```
        echo "Stopping container..."
        podman stop $CONTAINER_NAME
        ;;
    restart)
        echo "Restarting container..."
        podman restart $CONTAINER_NAME
        ;;
    status)
        podman ps -a | grep $CONTAINER_NAME
        ;;
    logs)
        podman logs -f $CONTAINER_NAME
        ;;
    *)
        echo "Usage: $0 {start|stop|restart|status|logs}"
        exit 1
        ;;
esac
chmod +x manage_podman_container.sh
```

Use the script to manage the Podman container:

```
./manage_podman_container.sh start
./manage_podman_container.sh status
./manage_podman_container.sh logs
```

Configure Environment Variables

Environment variables are crucial for configuring applications without hardcoding values.

Using Environment Variables in Docker

You can pass environment variables to Docker containers using the **-e** flag or an environment file.

- Option 1: Using the `-e` Flag

```
docker run -d -e VAR_NAME=value image_name
```

- Option 2: Using an Environment File

Create a file named **`.env`**:

```
DB_HOST=db.example.com
DB_USER=dbuser
DB_PASS=dbpassword
```

Modify **`run_container.sh`** to use the environment file:

```
# Define environment variables
ENV_FILE="--env-file .env"
docker run -d --name $CONTAINER_NAME -p 8080:8080 $ENV_FILE
$IMAGE_NAME:$IMAGE_TAG
```

Using Environment Variables in Podman

Podman accepts the same flags as Docker for environment variables.

- Option 1: Using the `-e` Flag

```
podman run -d -e VAR_NAME=value image_name
```

- Option 2: Using an Environment File

Modify **`run_podman_container.sh`**:

```
# Define environment variables
ENV_FILE="--env-file .env"
podman run -d --name $CONTAINER_NAME -p 8080:8080 $ENV_FILE
$IMAGE_NAME:$IMAGE_TAG
```

Automate Container Deployment across Environments

You can use scripts to specify environment-specific configurations to deploy containers in different environments (development, staging, production).

For this, create **.env.development**, **.env.staging**, and **.env.production** files with appropriate variables.

Then, update **run_container.sh**:

```
# Get the environment from the first argument
ENVIRONMENT=$1
if [ -z "$ENVIRONMENT" ]; then
    echo "Usage: $0 {development|staging|production}"
    exit 1
fi
ENV_FILE="--env-file .env.$ENVIRONMENT"
docker run -d --name $CONTAINER_NAME -p 8080:8080 $ENV_FILE
$IMAGE_NAME:$IMAGE_TAG
chmod +x run_container.sh
```

Run the script for the desired environment:

```
./run_container.sh development
```

Then, repeat similar changes for **run_podman_container.sh**.

By automating the process of building images, running containers, and managing configurations with Docker and Podman, we can ensure consistency across environments, reduce manual errors, and get things up and running faster.

Managing Containers and Orchestration

Building upon our previous scripts for container deployment, we now focus on managing containers more effectively using shell scripting. This includes tasks such as scaling containers up or down, accessing logs for monitoring, and implementing health checks to ensure containers are running optimally. By automating these tasks, we enhance our ability to orchestrate containers efficiently in various environments.

Scale Containers

Scaling involves adjusting the number of container instances to meet the demand. We can automate scaling by creating scripts that start or stop containers based on predefined criteria. Here, create a script named **scale_containers.sh**:

```
#!/bin/bash
IMAGE_NAME="myapp"
IMAGE_TAG="v1.0"
BASE_CONTAINER_NAME="myapp_instance"
START_PORT=8080
INSTANCES=$1
if [ -z "$INSTANCES" ]; then
    echo "Usage: $0 <number_of_instances>"
    exit 1
fi
echo "Scaling to $INSTANCES instances..."
# Stop and remove existing containers
EXISTING_CONTAINERS=$(docker ps -a -q --filter
"ancestor=$IMAGE_NAME:$IMAGE_TAG")
if [ ! -z "$EXISTING_CONTAINERS" ]; then
    echo "Stopping existing containers..."
    docker stop $EXISTING_CONTAINERS
    docker rm $EXISTING_CONTAINERS
fi
# Start new instances
for ((i=1; i<=INSTANCES; i++)); do
    PORT=$((START_PORT + i - 1))
    CONTAINER_NAME="${BASE_CONTAINER_NAME}_${i}"
    echo "Starting container $CONTAINER_NAME on port $PORT..."
    docker run -d --name $CONTAINER_NAME -p $PORT:8080
$IMAGE_NAME:$IMAGE_TAG
done
echo "Scaling completed."
```

Now, scale up to 3 instances:

```
./scale_containers.sh 3
```

This script stops any existing containers based on the image and starts the specified number of new instances, mapping them to sequential ports.

Access Container Logs

Monitoring logs is essential for diagnosing issues and ensuring that containers are functioning correctly. For this, create a script named **logs_containers.sh**:

```
#!/bin/bash
BASE_CONTAINER_NAME="myapp_instance"
if [ -z "$1" ]; then
    echo "Usage: $0 <instance_number|all>"
    exit 1
fi
if [ "$1" == "all" ]; then
    echo "Displaying logs for all containers..."
    CONTAINERS=$(docker ps --format "{{.Names}}" | grep
"$BASE_CONTAINER_NAME")
    for CONTAINER in $CONTAINERS; do
        echo "Logs for $CONTAINER:"
        docker logs $CONTAINER
        echo "-------------------------"
    done
else
    CONTAINER_NAME="${BASE_CONTAINER_NAME}_$1"
    echo "Displaying logs for $CONTAINER_NAME..."
    docker logs $CONTAINER_NAME
fi
```

View logs for a specific instance:

```
./logs_containers.sh 1
```

View logs for all instances:

```
./logs_containers.sh all
```

Implement Health Checks

Health checks help ensure that containers are operational and serving requests as expected.

First, modify the **Dockerfile** to include a health check instruction:

```
# ... existing Dockerfile content ...
# Define health check
HEALTHCHECK --interval=30s --timeout=5s --retries=3 \
  CMD curl -f http://localhost:8080/health || exit 1
```

This adds a health check that tries to access the **/health** endpoint every 30 seconds.

Next, create a script named **check_container_health.sh**:

```
#!/bin/bash
BASE_CONTAINER_NAME="myapp_instance"
CONTAINERS=$(docker ps --format "{{.Names}}" | grep
"$BASE_CONTAINER_NAME")
for CONTAINER in $CONTAINERS; do
    HEALTH_STATUS=$(docker inspect --
format='{{.State.Health.Status}}' $CONTAINER)
    echo "Container $CONTAINER health status: $HEALTH_STATUS"
done
./check_container_health.sh
```

This script retrieves and displays the health status of each container instance.

Manage Container Networking

Here, you can set up networking to let containers talk to each other or set up load balancing.

For this, create a script named **setup_network.sh**:

```
#!/bin/bash
```

```
NETWORK_NAME="myapp_network"
echo "Creating Docker network $NETWORK_NAME..."
docker network create $NETWORK_NAME
echo "Network $NETWORK_NAME created."
./setup_network.sh
```

Next, modify **scale_containers.sh** to connect containers to the network:

```
# ... existing content ...
NETWORK_NAME="myapp_network"
# Start new instances
for ((i=1; i<=INSTANCES; i++)); do
    PORT=$((START_PORT + i - 1))
    CONTAINER_NAME="${BASE_CONTAINER_NAME}_${i}"
    echo "Starting container $CONTAINER_NAME on port $PORT..."
    docker run -d --name $CONTAINER_NAME --network
$NETWORK_NAME -p $PORT:8080 $IMAGE_NAME:$IMAGE_TAG
done
```

Implement Load Balancing

Here, deploy an HAProxy container to distribute traffic among application containers.

- Creating HAProxy Configuration

```
global
    daemon
    maxconn 256
defaults
    mode http
    timeout connect 5000ms
    timeout client  50000ms
    timeout server  50000ms
```

```
frontend http-in
    bind *:80
    default_backend servers
backend servers
    balance roundrobin
{% for i in range(1, INSTANCES + 1) %}
    server app{{i}} myapp_instance_{{i}}:8080 check
{% endfor %}
```

Try using a templating engine like Jinja2 to generate the configuration based on the number of instances.

- Creating a Script to Deploy HAProxy Container

```
#!/bin/bash
INSTANCES=$1
if [ -z "$INSTANCES" ]; then
    echo "Usage: $0 <number_of_instances>"
    exit 1
fi
# Generate haproxy.cfg
CONFIG_FILE="haproxy.cfg"
echo "Generating HAProxy configuration..."
cat << EOF > $CONFIG_FILE
global
    daemon
    maxconn 256
defaults
    mode http
    timeout connect 5000ms
    timeout client  50000ms
    timeout server  50000ms
```

```
frontend http-in
    bind *:80
    default_backend servers
backend servers
    balance roundrobin
EOF
for ((i=1; i<=INSTANCES; i++)); do
    echo "    server app$i myapp_instance_$i:8080 check" >>
$CONFIG_FILE
done
# Run HAProxy container
echo "Deploying HAProxy container..."
docker run -d --name haproxy_container --network myapp_network
-p 80:80 \
    -v
$(pwd)/haproxy.cfg:/usr/local/etc/haproxy/haproxy.cfg:ro
haproxy:latest
echo "HAProxy deployed."
```

Next, scale the application containers:

```
./scale_containers.sh 3
```

Then, deploy HAProxy:

```
./deploy_haproxy.sh 3
```

Now, HAProxy will distribute incoming traffic on port 80 to the application containers.

Monitor Containers

You can automate the monitoring of container resource usage using scripts. To do this, just create a monitoring script and name it.**monitor_containers.sh**:

```
#!/bin/bash
```

```
CONTAINERS=$(docker ps --format "{{.Names}}" | grep
"myapp_instance")
echo "Monitoring container resource usage..."
for CONTAINER in $CONTAINERS; do
    echo "Stats for $CONTAINER:"
    docker stats $CONTAINER --no-stream
    echo "-------------------------"
done
./monitor_containers.sh
```

This script displays CPU and memory usage for each container.

We've automated a lot of important tasks by using shell scripting to manage containers and orchestration. This lets us handle complex container operations more efficiently, which means our applications are more available, resilient, and perform better.

Automating Kubernetes Deployment and Management

Kubernetes is an awesome platform for automating deployment, scaling, and management of containerized applications. You can use **kubectl**, the command-line tool for Kubernetes, to automate these tasks efficiently. In this section, we'll first install and configure **kubectl** in our existing environment. Then, we'll build upon our previous scripts to utilize **kubectl** for automating deployment, updates, and scaling within a Kubernetes cluster.

Install kubectl

- Download the latest release of **kubectl**:

```
curl -LO "https://storage.googleapis.com/kubernetes-
release/release/$(curl -s
https://storage.googleapis.com/kubernetes-
release/release/stable.txt)/bin/linux/amd64/kubectl"
```

- Make the Binary Executable

```
chmod +x ./kubectl
```

- Move the Binary to Your PATH

```
sudo mv ./kubectl /usr/local/bin/kubectl
kubectl version --client
```

You should see the client version information displayed.

Setting up a Kubernetes Cluster

For testing purposes, we will use **minikube**, which allows you to run a single-node Kubernetes cluster locally.

- Install Minikube Dependencies

```
sudo apt-get update
sudo apt-get install -y apt-transport-https ca-certificates
curl
```

- Download Minikube Binary

```
curl -Lo minikube
https://storage.googleapis.com/minikube/releases/latest/miniku
be-linux-amd64
chmod +x minikube
```

- Move the Binary to Your PATH

```
sudo mv minikube /usr/local/bin/
```

- Start Minikube

```
minikube start --driver=none
```

Remember that the **--driver=none** option allows Minikube to run directly on the host, but it requires root privileges.

- Verify the Cluster Status

```
kubectl cluster-info
```

You should also see information about the Kubernetes control plane and services.

Deploy Applications with 'kubectl'

- Create a Kubernetes Deployment Configuration

```yaml
apiVersion: apps/v1
kind: Deployment
metadata:
  name: myapp-deployment
spec:
  replicas: 3
  selector:
    matchLabels:
      app: myapp
  template:
    metadata:
      labels:
        app: myapp
    spec:
      containers:
      - name: myapp-container
        image: myapp:v1.0
        ports:
        - containerPort: 8080
        env:
        - name: DB_HOST
          value: "db.example.com"
        - name: DB_USER
          value: "dbuser"
        - name: DB_PASS
          value: "dbpassword"
```

- Create a Service Configuration

```
apiVersion: v1
kind: Service
metadata:
  name: myapp-service
spec:
  type: NodePort
  selector:
    app: myapp
  ports:
  - protocol: TCP
    port: 80
    targetPort: 8080
    nodePort: 30007
```

- Build and Push the Docker Image

Since Kubernetes pulls images from a registry, push your image to Docker Hub or a local registry.

```
docker tag myapp:v1.0 your_dockerhub_username/myapp:v1.0
```

- Push the Image

```
docker push your_dockerhub_username/myapp:v1.0
```

- Update the Deployment Configuration

Here, replace **`image: myapp:v1.0`** with **`image: your_dockerhub_username/myapp:v1.0`** in **`deployment.yaml`**.

- Deploy the Application

For this, create a script named **`deploy_k8s.sh`**:

```
#!/bin/bash
echo "Deploying application to Kubernetes..."
kubectl apply -f deployment.yaml
```

```
kubectl apply -f service.yaml
echo "Deployment initiated."
./deploy_k8s.sh
```

- Verify the Deployment

```
kubectl get deployments
kubectl get pods
kubectl get services
```

- Access the Application

First, find the Minikube IP:

```
minikube ip
```

Then, access the application at **`http://<minikube_ip>:30007`**.

Automate Updates

When a new version of the application is available, automate the update process.

- Build and push the new image

```
docker build -t your_dockerhub_username/myapp:v1.1 .
docker push your_dockerhub_username/myapp:v1.1
```

- Update the deployment configuration

```
# ... existing content ...
        image: your_dockerhub_username/myapp:v1.1
# ... existing content ...
```

- Create an update script

```
#!/bin/bash
echo "Updating application in Kubernetes..."
kubectl set image deployment/myapp-deployment myapp-
container=your_dockerhub_username/myapp:v1.1
```

```
echo "Update initiated."
./update_k8s.sh
```

- Verify the update

```
kubectl rollout status deployment/myapp-deployment
```

This command shows the status of the deployment update.

Automate Rollbacks

In case of issues with a new deployment, do automate rollbacks. For this, create a script named **rollback_k8s.sh**:

```
#!/bin/bash
echo "Rolling back the deployment..."
kubectl rollout undo deployment/myapp-deployment
echo "Rollback initiated."
./rollback_k8s.sh
```

Automate Health Checks

Kubernetes has the capability to automatically manage pod health. For this, modify **deployment.yaml** to include readiness and liveness probes:

```
# ... existing content ...
        livenessProbe:
          httpGet:
            path: /health
            port: 8080
          initialDelaySeconds: 15
          periodSeconds: 20
        readinessProbe:
          httpGet:
            path: /health
```

```
          port: 8080
        initialDelaySeconds: 5
        periodSeconds: 10
# ... existing content ...
```

Then, apply the updated configuration:

```
kubectl apply -f deployment.yaml
```

Verify the probes:

```
kubectl describe pods
```

Then you can look for **Liveness** and **Readiness** probe information.

Automate Resource Management

Make sure you set resource requests and limits so that you can be sure you're allocating resources fairly. Just update the deployment configuration by modifying it and you're all set!

```
# ... existing content ...
        resources:
          requests:
            cpu: "100m"
            memory: "200Mi"
          limits:
            cpu: "500m"
            memory: "500Mi"
# ... existing content ...
```

Then apply the changes:

```
kubectl apply -f deployment.yaml
```

Automate CI/CD Integration

You can use tools like Jenkins or GitLab CI to integrate Kubernetes deployment scripts into your CI/CD pipelines. Let us consider the following jenkins pipeline script:

```
pipeline {
    agent any
    stages {
        stage('Build') {
            steps {
                sh './build_image.sh'
            }
        }
        stage('Push') {
            steps {
                sh 'docker push
your_dockerhub_username/myapp:v1.0'
            }
        }
        stage('Deploy') {
            steps {
                sh './deploy_k8s.sh'
            }
        }
    }
}
```

We've integrated Kubernetes into our environment by installing and configuring **kubectl**. We've used shell scripts to automate the deployment, updates, and scaling of our application within a Kubernetes cluster. This automation makes it easier to manage containerized apps, letting you scale up quickly, deploy new versions rapidly, and apply updates consistently.

Summary

In general, we looked at what containerization can do and how shell scripting helps us manage containers. We started off by using scripts to deploy containers with Docker and Podman. This lets us automate the process of building images, running containers, and managing configurations with environment variables. This automation made sure everything was consistent across different environments and made the deployment process a lot more efficient, reducing the chance of human error.

Next, we looked at managing containers and orchestration with shell scripts. This included things like scaling containers up or down, accessing logs for monitoring, and implementing health checks to ensure optimal performance. I also showed you how to automate these tasks so you can orchestrate containers more effectively. Finally, I taught you how to automate Kubernetes deployment and management. I installed and configured kubectl and showed you how to use it to automate deployment, updates, and scaling within Kubernetes clusters. With this, you can handle complex cluster operations with ease, ensuring high availability and optimal resource utilization for your applications.

CHAPTER 9: DEVOPS SECURITY AUTOMATION WITH SHELL SCRIPTING

Overview

In this last chapter, we will look at using shell scripting to automate security practices in the DevOps workflow. First, we will go over how to script user access and permission management. I will show you how to automate the creation, modification, and deletion of user accounts and permissions. This way, you can make sure everyone's following the same security policies across all systems, and you can cut down on the risk of human error.

Next, we will look at automating vulnerability scanning and patching. We will also look at how to create scripts to detect security vulnerabilities and automate the application of patches and updates. This proactive approach keeps your systems safe by making sure they're all running the latest security fixes.

Finally, we will look at system audits and compliance checks. We will create scripts that automate the auditing of system configurations and make sure everything's compliant with the company's policies and industry regulations. The good thing about automating these checks is that we can regularly assess our security posture, identify any deviations, and take corrective actions promptly. By the end of this, we will have the skills we need to make our DevOps processes more secure. That way, we can be sure our systems are efficient, secure, and compliant.

Scripting User Access and Permissions Management

Keeping track of user accounts and permissions is a big part of system administration and security. Automating these tasks makes things more consistent, reduces the chance of manual errors, and makes it easier to onboard and offboard users. So now, we're going to learn how to automate user account setup, permission assignments, and access control using shell scripting for our project.

Automate User Account Setup

It can take a while to set up new user accounts by hand, particularly when there are lots of people to add. If we script the process, we can quickly add users with predefined settings.

```
#!/bin/bash

# Check if the script is run as root

if [[ $EUID -ne 0 ]]; then

   echo "This script must be run as root."

   exit 1

fi
```

```
# Check if a username is provided
if [[ -z "$1" ]]; then
    echo "Usage: $0 username [public_key_file]"
    exit 1
fi
USERNAME=$1
PASSWORD=$(openssl rand -base64 12)
HOME_DIR="/home/$USERNAME"
# Create the user with a home directory and bash shell
useradd -m -s /bin/bash "$USERNAME"
# Set the user's password
echo "$USERNAME:$PASSWORD" | chpasswd
# Expire the password to force change on first login
passwd --expire "$USERNAME"
echo "User $USERNAME has been created with a temporary
password."
# Optional: Set up SSH access with a public key
if [[ -n "$2" ]]; then
    PUBLIC_KEY_FILE=$2
    SSH_DIR="$HOME_DIR/.ssh"
    AUTH_KEYS="$SSH_DIR/authorized_keys"
    # Create .ssh directory and set permissions
    mkdir -p "$SSH_DIR"
    chmod 700 "$SSH_DIR"
    chown "$USERNAME:$USERNAME" "$SSH_DIR"
    # Copy the public key
    cp "$PUBLIC_KEY_FILE" "$AUTH_KEYS"
    chmod 600 "$AUTH_KEYS"
    chown "$USERNAME:$USERNAME" "$AUTH_KEYS"
```

```
    echo "SSH public key has been installed for $USERNAME."
fi
```

Now, to create a user without SSH key:

```
sudo ./create_user.sh john_doe
```

To create a user with an SSH public key:

```
sudo ./create_user.sh jane_doe /path/to/jane_doe.pub
```

Here,

- The script checks if it's run as root since creating users requires root privileges.
- It accepts a username and an optional public key file.
- A random temporary password is generated using **openssl**.
- The user is created with a home directory and the Bash shell.
- The password is set and then expired to force the user to change it on first login.
- If a public key is provided, it sets up SSH key-based authentication.

Automate Permission Assignment

It's key to make sure users have the right permissions so they can access only the resources they need.

So let us group users according to their roles to simplify permission management.

```
sudo groupadd developers
sudo groupadd testers
```

Then, update **create_user.sh** to include group assignment:

```
# ... existing script ...
# Check if a group is provided
if [[ -z "$3" ]]; then
    echo "No group specified. User will not be added to any specific group."
else
```

```
    GROUP=$3
    # Check if the group exists
    if grep -q "^$GROUP:" /etc/group; then
        usermod -aG "$GROUP" "$USERNAME"
        echo "User $USERNAME has been added to group $GROUP."
    else
        echo "Group $GROUP does not exist."
    fi
fi
```

Next, running the script with group assignment:

```
sudo ./create_user.sh alice /path/to/alice.pub developers
```

Then, create a script named **set_permissions.sh**:

```
#!/bin/bash
# Check if the script is run as root
if [[ $EUID -ne 0 ]]; then
   echo "This script must be run as root."
   exit 1
fi
# Define directories and groups
declare -A DIRS_GROUPS=(
    ["/var/www/project/app"]="developers"
    ["/var/www/project/test"]="testers"
)
# Set permissions
for DIR in "${!DIRS_GROUPS[@]}"; do
    GROUP="${DIRS_GROUPS[$DIR]}"
    chown -R :"$GROUP" "$DIR"
    chmod -R 770 "$DIR"
```

```
    echo "Permissions set for $DIR with group $GROUP."
done
```

Here,

- The script assigns group ownership and sets directory permissions recursively.
- **chmod 770** gives full permissions to the owner and group, and no permissions to others.

Automate Access Control

The next step is to set up access control lists (ACLs), which give you a lot of control over who can do what on your system. First thing's first: make sure the filesystem you're using supports ACLs. Most modern ones like ext4 do.

Then, you need to modify set_permissions.sh to use ACLs.

```
# ... existing script ...
# Set ACLs
for DIR in "${!DIRS_GROUPS[@]}"; do
    GROUP="${DIRS_GROUPS[$DIR]}"
    setfacl -Rm g:"$GROUP":rwx "$DIR"
    setfacl -dRm g:"$GROUP":rwx "$DIR"
    echo "ACLs set for $DIR with group $GROUP."
done
```

Here,

- **setfacl -Rm** sets ACLs recursively and modifies existing entries.
- **-d** sets default ACLs for new files and directories.
- This ensures that all existing and future files under the directories have the correct permissions.

Automate User Deactivation and Removal

Let's automate the process of deactivating or removing users when they leave the project. Just create a script and name it something like: **remove_user.sh**:

```
#!/bin/bash
```

```
# Check if the script is run as root
if [[ $EUID -ne 0 ]]; then
   echo "This script must be run as root."
   exit 1
fi
# Check if a username is provided
if [[ -z "$1" ]]; then
    echo "Usage: $0 username"
    exit 1
fi
USERNAME=$1
# Lock the user account
usermod -L "$USERNAME"
# Kill any running processes
pkill -u "$USERNAME"
echo "User $USERNAME has been locked and processes
terminated."
# Optional: Remove the user account and home directory
read -p "Do you want to remove the user account and home
directory? (y/n): " CONFIRM
if [[ "$CONFIRM" == "y" ]]; then
    userdel -r "$USERNAME"
    echo "User $USERNAME has been removed."
else
    echo "User $USERNAME has not been removed."
fi
```

Here,

- The script locks the user account and terminates any running processes.
- It prompts for confirmation before removing the user account and home directory.

- Locking the account prevents login without deleting user data immediately.

Automate SSH Key Management

Simply create a script named **update_ssh_keys.sh**:

```
#!/bin/bash
# Check if the script is run as root
if [[ $EUID -ne 0 ]]; then
   echo "This script must be run as root."
   exit 1
fi
# Check if username and key file are provided
if [[ -z "$1" || -z "$2" ]]; then
    echo "Usage: $0 username public_key_file"
    exit 1
fi
USERNAME=$1
PUBLIC_KEY_FILE=$2
HOME_DIR="/home/$USERNAME"
SSH_DIR="$HOME_DIR/.ssh"
AUTH_KEYS="$SSH_DIR/authorized_keys"
# Verify user exists
if ! id "$USERNAME" &>/dev/null; then
    echo "User $USERNAME does not exist."
    exit 1
fi
# Backup existing authorized_keys
if [[ -f "$AUTH_KEYS" ]]; then
    cp "$AUTH_KEYS" "${AUTH_KEYS}.bak_$(date +%F_%T)"
fi
```

```
# Update authorized_keys
cp "$PUBLIC_KEY_FILE" "$AUTH_KEYS"
chmod 600 "$AUTH_KEYS"
chown "$USERNAME:$USERNAME" "$AUTH_KEYS"
echo "SSH keys updated for $USERNAME."
sudo ./update_ssh_keys.sh alice /path/to/new_alice.pub
```

Here,

- The script updates the **authorized_keys** file for the specified user.
- It backs up the existing **authorized_keys** before making changes.

Automate Password Policy Enforcement

Make sure users stick to the company password policy. Write a script and name it something simple, like **enforce_password_policy.sh**:

```
#!/bin/bash
# Install required package
sudo apt-get install libpam-pwquality -y
# Configure password policy
PWQUALITY_CONF="/etc/security/pwquality.conf"
sudo sed -i 's/^# minlen = .*/minlen = 12/' "$PWQUALITY_CONF"
sudo sed -i 's/^# dcredit = .*/dcredit = -1/'
"$PWQUALITY_CONF"
sudo sed -i 's/^# ucredit = .*/ucredit = -1/'
"$PWQUALITY_CONF"
sudo sed -i 's/^# ocredit = .*/ocredit = -1/'
"$PWQUALITY_CONF"
sudo sed -i 's/^# lcredit = .*/lcredit = -1/'
"$PWQUALITY_CONF"
echo "Password policy enforced: minimum length 12, requires
uppercase, lowercase, digit, and special character."
```

Here,

- The script installs **libpam-pwquality**, which enforces password complexity requirements.
- It updates **/etc/security/pwquality.conf** to set minimum length and character type requirements.

Automate Audit of User Accounts

Keeping on top of auditing user accounts is a great way to keep security in check. It's a good idea to create a script called **audit_users.sh**:

```
#!/bin/bash
echo "Listing all user accounts:"
cut -d: -f1 /etc/passwd
echo -e "\nUsers with UID 0 (should only be root):"
awk -F: '($3 == "0") {print $1}' /etc/passwd
echo -e "\nAccounts with empty passwords:"
awk -F: '($2 == "") {print $1}' /etc/shadow
echo -e "\nLocked accounts:"
passwd -S -a | grep " L "
echo -e "\nLast login times:"
lastlog
```

Here, the script provides information about user accounts, helping identify any anomalies.

All these above scripts help maintain consistent configurations, enforce security policies, and simplify user management tasks. The automation of these processes reduces the risk of human error, ensures compliance with organizational policies, and allows system administrators to focus on more strategic activities.

Automating Vulnerability Scanning and Patching

Given the need to be on the ball with keeping systems secure, it's important that you regularly scan for weaknesses and apply patches without delay. Automating these processes makes sure that security measures are consistently applied, reducing the window of exposure to potential threats. In a nutshell, we'll be building scripts to automate security scans, vulnerability checks, and patch deployments.

Automate Security Scans

Security scans help identify weaknesses in systems that could be exploited. Tools like **OpenSCAP**, **Lynis**, and **Nessus** can be used for scanning. OpenSCAP is an open-source tool that provides a standardized approach for maintaining the security of enterprise systems.

- Installing OpenSCAP

```
sudo apt-get update
sudo apt-get install -y openscap-utils
```

- Downloading Security Content

Security Content Automation Protocol (SCAP) content provides policies and checks.

```
wget
https://www.redhat.com/security/data/oval/com.redhat.rhsa-all.xml
```

- Creating a Security Scan Script

Now here, create a script named **`security_scan.sh`**:

```
#!/bin/bash
# Define variables
REPORT_DIR="/var/reports/security"
TIMESTAMP=$(date +"%Y%m%d_%H%M%S")
REPORT_FILE="$REPORT_DIR/security_scan_$TIMESTAMP.html"
# Create report directory if it doesn't exist
mkdir -p "$REPORT_DIR"
# Perform the scan
oscap xccdf eval --profile
xccdf_org.ssgproject.content_profile_pci-dss \
    --results "$REPORT_DIR/results_$TIMESTAMP.xml" \
    --report "$REPORT_FILE" \
    /usr/share/openscap/scap-yast2sec.xml
```

```
echo "Security scan completed. Report saved to $REPORT_FILE"
```

Here,

- The script uses **oscap xccdf eval** to evaluate the system against the specified security profile.
- Reports are saved with timestamps for record-keeping.

Automate Vulnerability Checks

You can set up your system to check for known vulnerabilities automatically using tools like Lynis.

```
sudo apt-get install -y lynis
```

Then, create a script named **vulnerability_check.sh**:

```
#!/bin/bash
# Define variables
REPORT_DIR="/var/reports/lynis"
TIMESTAMP=$(date +"%Y%m%d_%H%M%S")
REPORT_FILE="$REPORT_DIR/lynis_report_$TIMESTAMP.txt"
# Create report directory if it doesn't exist
mkdir -p "$REPORT_DIR"
# Run Lynis audit
sudo lynis audit system --quiet --logfile
"$REPORT_DIR/lynis.log" --report-file "$REPORT_FILE"
echo "Vulnerability check completed. Report saved to
$REPORT_FILE"
```

Here, Lynis performs an in-depth system audit and generates a report which are saved with timestamps for tracking.

You can then schedule the vulnerability check to run weekly:

```
sudo crontab -e
0 3 * * 1 /path/to/vulnerability_check.sh
```

This schedules the check to run every Monday at 3 AM.

Automate Patch Deployment

It's really important to make sure that your systems are up to date with the latest patches to keep them secure.

```
#!/bin/bash
# Check if the script is run as root
if [[ $EUID -ne 0 ]]; then
   echo "This script must be run as root."
   exit 1
fi
echo "Updating package lists..."
sudo apt-get update -y
echo "Upgrading packages..."
sudo apt-get upgrade -y
echo "Cleaning up..."
sudo apt-get autoremove -y
sudo apt-get clean
echo "System patched successfully."
```

The script is great for keeping package lists up to date, upgrading packages, and cleaning up any unnecessary files. If you run this script on a regular basis, it'll make sure your system is running with the latest security patches.

You can also schedule the patch deployment to run weekly:

```
sudo crontab -e
0 4 * * 1 /path/to/deploy_patches.sh
```

This schedules the patch deployment to run every Monday at 4 AM.

Automate Notifications

You can set up email notifications to alert administrators about the results of scans and updates.

```
sudo apt-get install -y mailutils
```

Just simply modify **security_scan.sh**:

```
# ... existing script ...
# Send email notification
mail -s "Security Scan Completed" admin@example.com <
"$REPORT_FILE"
```

Then modify **vulnerability_check.sh**:

```
# ... existing script ...
# Send email notification
mail -s "Vulnerability Check Completed" admin@example.com <
"$REPORT_FILE"
```

Modify this **deploy_patches.sh** as well:

```
# ... existing script ...
# Send email notification
echo "System patched successfully on $(date)" | mail -s "Patch
Deployment Completed" admin@example.com
```

After each operation, an email is sent to the administrator with the report or confirmation.

Automate System Reboots After Patching

Some patches may require a system reboot, which ca n be done by simply modifying **deploy_patches.sh**:

```
# ... existing script ...
# Check if a reboot is required
if [ -f /var/run/reboot-required ]; then
    echo "System reboot is required. Rebooting now..."
    sudo reboot
else
    echo "No reboot required."
fi
```

The script then checks for the presence of **/var/run/reboot-required** to determine if a reboot is necessary.

Automate Vulnerability Scanning for Containers

You can use tools like Clair or Anchore to scan container images for vulnerabilities. To get started, you'll want to run the Anchore Engine using Docker Compose.

Just create a script named **scan_container.sh**:

```
pip install anchorecli


#!/bin/bash
IMAGE_NAME="your_dockerhub_username/myapp:v1.0"
# Add the image to Anchore
anchore-cli image add $IMAGE_NAME
# Wait for analysis to complete
echo "Waiting for analysis to complete..."
sleep 60
# Get the vulnerability report
anchore-cli image vuln $IMAGE_NAME all >
container_vuln_report.txt
echo "Container vulnerability scan completed. Report saved to
container_vuln_report.txt"
# Send email notification
mail -s "Container Vulnerability Scan Completed"
admin@example.com < container_vuln_report.txt
```

The script adds the image to Anchore Engine, waits for analysis, and retrieves the vulnerability report.

Automate Log Monitor for Security Events

You can use tools like OSSEC or Wazuh to monitor logs for any security events that might come up. Just follow the installation guide over at OSSEC Documentation, then set up email alerts in the OSSEC configuration with a script named **monitor_security_events.sh**:

```
#!/bin/bash
```

```
# Check for security events

grep -i "security" /var/ossec/logs/alerts/alerts.log >
recent_security_events.txt

if [ -s recent_security_events.txt ]; then

    echo "Security events detected. Sending email
notification."

    mail -s "Security Events Detected" admin@example.com <
recent_security_events.txt

else

    echo "No security events detected."

fi
```

Then schedule the script to run hourly:

```
sudo crontab -e

0 * * * * /path/to/monitor_security_events.sh
```

Automate Firewall Configuration

You also ensure firewall rules are consistently applied.

```
#!/bin/bash

# Check if the script is run as root

if [[ $EUID -ne 0 ]]; then

   echo "This script must be run as root."

   exit 1

fi

echo "Configuring UFW firewall..."

# Reset UFW to default settings

ufw reset

# Deny all incoming connections by default

ufw default deny incoming

# Allow all outgoing connections
```

```
ufw default allow outgoing
# Allow SSH
ufw allow ssh
# Allow specific ports (e.g., HTTP and HTTPS)
ufw allow http
ufw allow https
# Enable UFW
ufw --force enable
echo "Firewall configuration completed."
```

The above script then configures UFW with common security best practices.

Automate Security Policy Enforcement

You can use tools like Ansible to make sure your servers have the right security settings in place. To do this, just create a playbook with the name **security.yml**:

```
---
- name: Apply security configurations
  hosts: all
  become: yes
  tasks:
    - name: Ensure UFW is installed
      apt:
        name: ufw
        state: present
    - name: Configure UFW
      ufw:
        rule: allow
        port: "{{ item }}"
    loop:
      - ssh
```

```
      - http
      - https
  - name: Set default policies
    command: ufw default deny incoming
  - command: ufw default allow outgoing
  - name: Enable UFW
    ufw:
      state: enabled
      logging: on
ansible-playbook -i inventory.ini security.yml
```

The playbook then applies firewall configurations across all specified hosts.

Putting these scripts on a regular maintenance schedule helps keep the company's security up to date and protects its assets and data from getting into the wrong hands.

System Audits and Compliance Checks

Overview

It's really important to make sure that our systems are compliant with the company policies and industry regulations. That's the best way to keep things secure and efficient. Having automated audits and compliance checks in place makes sure that systems stick to the rules, spots any issues right away, and gets them fixed quickly. In this section, we'll build on what we've learned before to write automated scripts for audits that log and verify system configurations. This will help us keep our systems in line with the rules and maintain compliance.

Before you start writing scripts, it's important to understand the compliance frameworks that apply to your organization. There are a few common frameworks you might come across:

- **CIS Benchmarks**: Best practices for secure system configurations.
- **PCI DSS**: Standards for organizations that handle credit card information.
- **HIPAA**: Regulations for protecting sensitive patient health information.
- **Internal Policies**: Organization-specific security and operational policies.

Using OpenSCAP for Compliance Checks

OpenSCAP is an open-source tool that provides automated compliance auditing based on SCAP (Security Content Automation Protocol) standards.

- Installing OpenSCAP

```
sudo apt-get update
sudo apt-get install -y libopenscap8 openscap-scanner
```

- Obtaining SCAP Security Guide

The SCAP Security Guide (SSG) provides security policies in SCAP format.

```
sudo apt-get install -y ssg-base ssg-debderived
```

- Identifying the Appropriate Profile

```
oscap info /usr/share/xml/scap/ssg/content/ssg-ubuntu1804-
ds.xml
```

Here, you must ensure that you replace **ubuntu1804** with your distribution version.

- Creating an Audit Script

Create a script named **audit_compliance.sh**:

```
#!/bin/bash
# Define variables
PROFILE="xccdf_org.ssgproject.content_profile_cis"
CONTENT_PATH="/usr/share/xml/scap/ssg/content/ssg-ubuntu1804-
ds.xml"
REPORT_DIR="/var/reports/compliance"
TIMESTAMP=$(date +"%Y%m%d_%H%M%S")
RESULTS_FILE="$REPORT_DIR/results_$TIMESTAMP.xml"
REPORT_FILE="$REPORT_DIR/compliance_report_$TIMESTAMP.html"
# Create report directory if it doesn't exist
mkdir -p "$REPORT_DIR"
# Perform the compliance check
oscap xccdf eval --profile $PROFILE \
    --results "$RESULTS_FILE" \
```

```
    --report "$REPORT_FILE" \
    $CONTENT_PATH
echo "Compliance audit completed. Report saved to
$REPORT_FILE"
# Send email notification (optional)
# mail -s "Compliance Audit Completed" admin@example.com <
"$REPORT_FILE"
sudo ./audit_compliance.sh
```

In the above script,

- The script runs an OpenSCAP evaluation against the selected profile.
- Reports are saved with timestamps for tracking over time.
- An HTML report provides a detailed overview of compliance status.

Automate Configuration Verification

Write up scripts to check specific system settings, such as SSH options, password policies, and firewall rules.

Consider an example of Verifying SSH Configuration. So for this, you create a script named **verify_ssh_config.sh**:

```
#!/bin/bash
CONFIG_FILE="/etc/ssh/sshd_config"
REPORT_FILE="/var/reports/audit/ssh_config_audit.txt"
# Create report directory if it doesn't exist
mkdir -p "$(dirname "$REPORT_FILE")"
echo "SSH Configuration Audit - $(date)" > "$REPORT_FILE"
echo "-----------------------------------" >> "$REPORT_FILE"
# Check for protocol version
if grep -q "^Protocol 2" "$CONFIG_FILE"; then
    echo "Protocol version is set to 2: PASS" >>
"$REPORT_FILE"
```

```
else
    echo "Protocol version is not set to 2: FAIL" >>
"$REPORT_FILE"
fi
# Check for root login
if grep -q "^PermitRootLogin no" "$CONFIG_FILE"; then
    echo "Root login is disabled: PASS" >> "$REPORT_FILE"
else
    echo "Root login is not disabled: FAIL" >> "$REPORT_FILE"
fi
# Check for password authentication
if grep -q "^PasswordAuthentication no" "$CONFIG_FILE"; then
    echo "Password authentication is disabled: PASS" >>
"$REPORT_FILE"
else
    echo "Password authentication is not disabled: FAIL" >>
"$REPORT_FILE"
fi
echo "SSH configuration audit completed. Report saved to
$REPORT_FILE"
sudo ./verify_ssh_config.sh
```

The above script checks for compliance with specific SSH configuration settings. Results are logged to a report file, indicating PASS or FAIL for each check.

Collect System Configuration Data

We can also automate the collection of configuration files and settings for audit purposes.

```
#!/bin/bash
OUTPUT_DIR="/var/reports/configs"
TIMESTAMP=$(date +"%Y%m%d_%H%M%S")
# Create output directory
```

```
mkdir -p "$OUTPUT_DIR"
# List of configuration files to collect
CONFIG_FILES=(
    "/etc/ssh/sshd_config"
    "/etc/passwd"
    "/etc/group"
    "/etc/sudoers"
    "/etc/security/pwquality.conf"
    "/etc/fstab"
    "/etc/hosts.allow"
    "/etc/hosts.deny"
)
# Copy configuration files
for FILE in "${CONFIG_FILES[@]}"; do
    if [[ -f "$FILE" ]]; then
        cp "$FILE" "$OUTPUT_DIR/$(basename
"$FILE")_$TIMESTAMP"
    fi
done
echo "System configuration files collected in $OUTPUT_DIR"
sudo ./collect_system_configs.sh
```

The script copies specified configuration files to a secure directory with timestamps. This aids in tracking changes over time and facilitates audits.

Compare Configurations Against Baselines

Set up some standard settings and then check to see if anything has been changed without permission. Once you've set up your system to comply with the standards, save the configuration files as a baseline.

```
sudo cp -r /var/reports/configs /var/reports/baseline_configs
```

Create a comparison script named **compare_configs.sh**:

```
#!/bin/bash
BASELINE_DIR="/var/reports/baseline_configs"
CURRENT_DIR="/var/reports/configs"
REPORT_FILE="/var/reports/audit/config_diff_report.txt"
# Create report directory if it doesn't exist
mkdir -p "$(dirname "$REPORT_FILE")"
echo "Configuration Difference Report - $(date)" >
"$REPORT_FILE"
echo "------------------------------------------" >>
"$REPORT_FILE"
for FILE in "$BASELINE_DIR"/*; do
    BASENAME=$(basename "$FILE")
    CURRENT_FILE="$CURRENT_DIR/$BASENAME"
    if [[ -f "$CURRENT_FILE" ]]; then
        DIFF_OUTPUT=$(diff "$FILE" "$CURRENT_FILE")
        if [[ -n "$DIFF_OUTPUT" ]]; then
            echo "Differences found in $BASENAME:" >>
"$REPORT_FILE"
            echo "$DIFF_OUTPUT" >> "$REPORT_FILE"
            echo "----------------------------------" >>
"$REPORT_FILE"
        else
            echo "No differences in $BASENAME: PASS" >>
"$REPORT_FILE"
        fi
    else
        echo "$BASENAME not found in current configurations:
FAIL" >> "$REPORT_FILE"
    fi
done
```

```
echo "Configuration comparison completed. Report saved to
$REPORT_FILE"
```

```
sudo ./collect_system_configs.sh
sudo ./compare_configs.sh
```

The script compares current configuration files against the baseline. The differences are logged for review, indicating potential unauthorized changes.

Schedule Regular Audits

We can also make use of CRON to schedule regular execution of audit scripts.

```
# Collect configurations daily at 1 AM
0 1 * * * /path/to/collect_system_configs.sh
# Run configuration comparison daily at 2 AM
0 2 * * * /path/to/compare_configs.sh
```

We can simply add the above entries to schedule the scripts.

Secure Audit Data

Let's say our goal is to make sure that audit reports and the data we collect is kept secure. For this, you can simply set the appropriate permissions:

```
chmod -R 600 /var/reports
chown -R root:root /var/reports
```

With this, only authorized personnel should have access to audit data.

All these scripts provide continuous monitoring, early detection of deviations, and facilitate timely corrective actions. All these regular audits, combined with effective response strategies, help maintain adherence to internal policies and external regulations, safeguarding the organization against security breaches and compliance violations.

Summary

In general, we tried to make security practices more automated in the DevOps workflow using shell scripting. We started off by automating user access and permissions management. We created scripts to handle user account setups, group assignments, and access controls. This automation made sure that security policies were the same across all systems, made it easier to get new people started and let them leave, and cut down on the chance of mistakes being made by people. We were able to improve the security of our systems and make sure that we were following the rules by managing permissions and enforcing our password policies through scripts.

Next, we automated the vulnerability scanning and patching process. We put together scripts to run regular security scans using tools like OpenSCAP and Lynis, automated the deployment of patches, and set up notifications for critical updates. This meant that potential threats couldn't reach our systems for long, and we kept everything up to date with the latest security fixes. Last but not least, we automated system audits and compliance checks. We created some scripts to make sure that our systems were set up correctly and that we were following all of the relevant rules and regulations.

Index

A

ACLs ... 152
Ansible ... 79, 111, 163
apt-get ... 100, 101, 102, 103, 104, 117, 121, 122, 123, 139, 155, 157, 158, 159, 160, 165
AWS CLI ... 69

B

Bandwidth Usage ... 100, 102
Bash ... 2, 3, 4, 5, 16, 21, 25, 34, 150

C

CI/CD ... 2, 20, 21, 24, 25, 27, 28, 29, 30, 32, 33, 34, 36, 40, 42, 43, 47, 48, 145
CIS Benchmarks ... 164
Compliance Checks ... 164, 165
Configuration Management ... 74, 111
Container Deployment ... 121, 123, 126, 131
Container Management ... 125, 128
Containerization ... 120
CRON Jobs ... 59, 63

D

Database Maintenance ... 93
Disk Usage ... 5
Docker ... 121, 122, 123, 124, 125, 130, 131, 135, 141, 146, 161
Documentation ... 80, 161

E

Environment Variables . 28, 38, 59, 124, 127, 129, 130
Error Handling ... 11

F

Firewall Configuration ... 77, 162
Functions ... 6, 16

G

Git ... 26, 27, 30, 31, 49, 69, 72, 80, 83, 84
GitHub ... 81

H

HAProxy ... 104, 105, 106, 107, 108, 111, 113, 114, 115, 119, 135, 136, 137, 138
Health Checks ... 58, 113, 134, 143
HIPAA ... 164

I

iftop ... 99, 100
Incident Detection ... 86
Incident Resolution ... 85, 86, 90, 93

J

Jinja2 ... 136
JSON ... 29, 51, 116

K

Keepalived ... 117
kubectl ... 138, 139, 140, 142, 143, 144, 145, 146
Kubernetes ... 121, 138, 139, 140, 141, 142, 143, 145, 146

L

Load Balancing ... 98, 135
Log Collection ... 94
Log Management ... 85, 97
Log Rotation ... 58
Logging ... 9, 11, 33
Lynis ... 157, 158, 171

M

Minikube ... 139, 140, 142
Monitoring ... 56, 60, 99, 100, 102, 114, 133, 138

N

netstat ... 99, 100, 101
Network Traffic ... 98, 99
nload ... 99

O

OpenSCAP ... 157, 165, 166

Orchestration 73, 74, 131

P

PCI DSS 164
Podman ... 121, 122, 123, 126, 127, 128, 129, 130, 131, 146

R

Resource Allocation 91
Resource Management 144
Rollbacks 29, 143

S

SCAP 157, 165
Security Automation 147
Service Restart 90
SSH 24, 27, 28, 30, 31, 72, 149, 150, 154, 155, 163, 166, 167
SSH Configuration 166
SSH Key Management 154
System Audits 164
System Metrics 86

T

Task Scheduling 56
tcpdump 99, 101
Terraform 79, 111
top 34, 62, 84, 87, 90, 104, 119, 156
Traffic Monitoring 99
Traffic Redirection 113

U

UFW 162, 163, 164
User Deactivation 152
User Session Management 93

V

Version Control 30, 80
vnStat 103, 104
VRRP 117
Vulnerability Scanning 156, 161

Y

YAML 27

Epilogue

As we wrap up this project, I hope the tools and techniques you've learned in this book become a regular part of your daily DevOps routine. The automation skills you've picked up are going to save you time and also make your workflows more reliable and efficient. When you script routine tasks, you free up your mind to focus on new ideas and problem-solving.

The world of DevOps moves pretty fast, so being able to adapt and make changes quickly is really important. The scripts and strategies we've talked about are meant to be practical tools you can start using right away. These skills can be used to automate deployments, manage configurations, and enhance security—and they can be applied to the challenges you face every day.

Remember, the shell is more than just a tool—it's there to help you get things done faster and more efficiently. Make the most of automation to transform the way you work on your projects. The skills you've learned are not just for the tasks at hand, but will help you grow and succeed in the ever-changing world of DevOps.

Thank You

www.ingramcontent.com/pod-product-compliance
Lightning Source LLC
Chambersburg PA
CBHW080213170726
48282CB00030B/1104
9788197950421